By same author

Tankhem: Seth & Egyptian Magick
The Bull of Ombos (Seth & Egyptian Magick II)
Supernatural Assault in Ancient Egypt
The Ritual Year in Ancient Egypt
Egyptian Magick: a spirited guide

Frontispiece: Dendera B, one of several famous circular astronomical ceilings from Dendara, now in the Louvre. It uses the native system of decans, as well as the Greco-Babylonian signs of the zodiac.

Demonic Calendar
of Ancient Egypt

Copyright © Mogg Morgan 2021

First paperback Edition

revised 2024

All rights reserved. No part of this work may be reproduced or utilized in any form by any means electronic or mechanical, including *xerography, photocopying, microfilm,* and *recording,* or by any information storage system without permission in writing from the publishers.

Published by

Mandrake

BM Mandrake, London

"The snake is in my hand
and cannot bite me"
Coffin Text 885

"Oh lion and serpent who destroys the
destroyer, be mighty among us"
Gnostic Mass

"I'll protect you from the hooded claw, keep
the vampire from your door."

Contents

Magical work how to use this Calendar & spells it contains 9
Invocation of the five gods 10
Standard opening rite (heptagram) 13
The lunar-stellar Year 15
The lunar calendar 16
Sirius & the Lunar-Stellar Calendar 20
The Lunar month 22
Some useful definitions for understanding Lunar calendars 23
The First Month of the Lunar Year 24
The Northern Lunar-Solar Winter Solstice Version 25
The South Lunar-Stellar
    or Lunar-Sothic Calendar Summer solstice (preferred) 28

The Demonic Calendar 37
The decans 37
What is a demon? 37
The demonic calendar 40
The star goddess 44
The book of Nwt 47
The Egyptian decans 50

Lucky & Unlucky days 53
Spells of protection & propitiation 128

The Demonic Calendar After the Pharaohs 131
decans of western astrology their meaning 131
A Case Study 133

Decans of Western Astrology (Compendium)
28. The First Decan of Aries 139
29. Second Decan of Aries 142
30. Third decan of Aries 144
31. First decan of Taurus 147
32. Second Decan of Taurus 150

33. Third Decan of Taurus 152
34. First Decan of Gemini 157
35. Second Decan of Gemini 160
36. Third Decan of Gemini 162
1. First Decan of Cancer 164
2. Second Decan of Cancer 167
3. Third Decan of Cancer 169
4. First Decan of Leo 171
5. Second Decan of Leo 174
6. Third Decan of Leo 176
7. First Decan of Virgo 178
8. Second Decan of Virgo 181
9. Third Decan of Virgo 183
10. First Decan of Libra 185
11. Second Decan of Libra 188
12. Third Decan of Libra 190
13. First Decan of Scorpio 192
14. Second Decan of Scorpio 195
15. Third Decan of Scorpio 197
16. First Decan of Sagittarius 199
17. Second Decan of Sagittarius 202
18. Third Decan of Sagittarius 204
19. First Decan of Capricorn 206
20. Second Decan of Capricorn 209
21. Third Decan of Capricorn 211
22. First Decan of Aquarius 213
23. Second Decan of Aquarius 216
24. Third Decan of Aquarius 218
25. First Decan of Pisces 220
26. Second Decan of Pisces 223
27. Third Decan of Pisces 225

Ephemeris of Lunar months 227
Index 229

Magical work how to use this Calendar & spells it contains

Mostly I would look at the decans as they come and go through the year, reading and reflecting upon the associated oracles. Some of these oracles seem to have ritual instructions, sometimes quite brief, for example the 16th Decan "Apply your heart to your local gods; propitiate your spirits (akhw); exalt your crew during the day on this day." Sometimes there is a more complex ritual that I think we can use in several different ways. In my book *Supernatural Assault in Ancient Egypt* I described how amulets were often made that enlisted the power of the god to counteract or perhaps mitigate against those very same gods, Thus we saw an amuletic decree utilising the power of the moon god Khonsu, to protect against a whole list of bad influences including Khonsu. Perhaps this is parallel to the way *Shitala*, "She Who Is Cool", the popular Hindu goddess of smallpox is worshipped! Some of the most magical deities often have this ambiguous character.

Invocation of the five gods

Make an amulet or sigil. The original rubrik says this should be worn for five days, so you could do that or, as I would more likely do, keep it on the altar for five days. From the fragmentary description, it looks like the amulet shows images of the five gods. The easiest way to do would be to use the hieroglyphs of the five, as in the picture overleaf:

REPEAT THE APPROPRIATE VERSES FROM THE SPELL AS YOU MAKE YOUR RITUAL GESTURES. ONE FOR EACH DAY OR ALL FIVE AND THE VALEDICTION ON THE FINAL DAY.

FIRST: THE BIRTH OF OSIRIS. WORDS TO BE SAID ON IT:

O Osiris, bull in his cavern (whose) name is hidden . Bull of his mother Nwt. Hail to thee, hail to thee . I am (thy offspring)... O father, Osiris.

FOR THE NAME OF THIS DAY: THE PURE ONE OF THE FIELD

SECOND: THE BIRTH OF HORUS. WORDS TO BE SAID ON IT :

O Horus, (*khenty-irty*) of Letopolis. It is repeated anew mighty of strength, master of fear, save me from bad and evil things and from any slaughter. Horus, son of Geb

THE NAME OF THIS DAY: POWERFUL IS THE HEART

THIRD: THE BIRTH OF SETH. WORDS TO BE SAID ON IT:

OH, SETH, Son of Nwt, great of strength, save me from bad and evil things and from any slaughter, protection is in thy, the hands of thy holiness. I am the offspring of your offspring.

THE NAME OF THE DAY : It is powerful of heart.

FOURTH : THE BIRTH OF ISIS. WORDS TO BE SAID ON IT:

Oh, Isis, daughter of Nwt, the eldest, mistress of magic, provider of the book, mistress who appeases the two lands, your face is glorious. I am your brother and your sister.

THE NAME OF THE DAY : SHE WHO MAKES TERROR.

FIFTH : THE BIRTH OF NEPHTHYS. WORDS TO BE SAID ON IT :

Oh, Nephthys, daughter of Nwt, sister of Seth, whose father sees a healthy daughter, beautiful of face. I am the divine power in the womb of my mother Nwt.

THE NAME OF THE DAY: The child who is in his nest.

FINAL WORDS (VALEDICTION)

WORDS TO BE SAID AFTER THEM WHEN THE EPAGOMENAL DAYS (OR DIFFICULT DAYS) ARE COMPLETED.

Hail to you! O great ones according to your names, children of a goddess who have come forth from the sacred womb, lords because of your father, goddesses because of your mother, without knowing the necropolis. Behold, may you protect (me) and save me. May you make me prosperous, may you make protection, may you repeat and may you protect me. I am one who is on your agenda.

THIS SPELL IS TO BE SAID FOUR TIMES.

STANDARD OPENING RITE (heptagram)

Hekas, Hekas, Este Babaloi
"Love and do what you will"

Face North and try to see the constellation
Ursa Major.
Draw down its power and say:

0. Guardians of the House of Life at Abydos
   Before me in the East: Nephthys
   Behind me in the West, Isis
   On my right hand in the South is Seth
   And on my left hand, in the North, Horus
   For above me shines the body of Nuit
   And below me extends the ground of Geb
   And in my centre abideth the 'Great Hidden God'

   Mnemonic:
   [FAther GEt GAme to FEEd the HOt NEw hOme]

1. Now turn to the East.

   Make the "Horus Fighting" gesture.

   [Breath in and in one perfect movement, form both hands into fists and raise them up and to the left of your head, stretch your right hand and arm in front of you and bring the left hand and arm to join it. As you finish the intonation, bring both hands back to the centre of your body]

   Vibrate the first vowel long and hard - AAAAAAA - as in fAther

2. Now turn to the North

Make the gesture "Horus Fighting" and vibrate the second vowel EEEEEEE, E as in gEt as above.

3. Then turn to the West

   Make the "Horus Fighting" gesture
   and vibrate ÊÊÊÊÊÊÊ, Ay as in GAme

4. Turn to the South

   Make the "Horus Fighting" gesture
   and vibrate IIIIIII, EE as in fEEd

5. Return to face the East

   Now bend over and reach out to the Earth
   vibrating OOOOOOO, as in HOt

6. Then gradually unfolding, come up and place your hands on your heart and vibrate YYYYYY - Ew as in NEw

7. Finally stretching up to the heavens
   vibrate Ô Ô Ô Ô Ô Ô Ô O as in HÔme.

   Now make the sign of the (invoking) pentagram in the air in front of you and vibrate

   > Aa, Eye, EE, Ou, Uh (Ay EAO - Oh Hail) Nephthys
   > Aa, Eye, EE, Ou, Uh (Ay EAO - Oh Hail) Horus
   > Aa, Eye, EE, Ou, Uh (Ay EAO - Oh Hail) Isis
   > Aa, Eye, EE, Ou, Uh (Ay EAO - Oh Hail) Seth
   > Aa, Eye, EE, Ou, Uh (Ay EAO - Oh Hail) Geb
   > Aa, Eye, EE, Ou, Uh (Ay EAO - Oh Hail) Nuit
   > Aa, Eye, EE, Ou, Uh (Ay EAO - Oh Hail) Hidden God

8. Repeat "Abydos Arrangement" (0)

The lunar-stellar Year

The demonic calendar that is the main subject of this book is lunar. Therefore, in order to understand the comings and goings of demons, one needs to know something about how this lunar calendar actually functions. The ten day rule of each demon does not occur on the same date each year but is fixed according to simple lunar observations. Without this, the inquirer has to make use of an almanac or ephemeris prepared each year, in advance, by someone who does know the rules. Such an ephemeris is available but it is still useful to know how it is compiled, in case you want to make your own.

Before setting out these components, I must first briefly recap the nature of the entire ritual year of those times. This is the backdrop for the changing matrix of decanal demons or daemons that come and go through the year. Anyone who attempts to reconstruct the working systems of ancient Egypt will have to make some assumptions about how these things worked. Different initial assumptions would lead to slight variations in the cycle. Whatever way one looks at it this is always going to be an approximation, but this one works for me. I hope it is also a dogma that will help you interpret your own experiences. I claim nothing more than that this should turn out to be a working system that fits the reader's experience.

It is now universally accepted that as measurements of time, the day and the lunar month arose in ancient cultures long before the concept of the year. Which means the very oldest Egyptian ritual calendar has to have been lunar. Somehow this all got submerged under a mass of newer stuff, which is one of the reasons why I want to try and reconstruct that lost lunar calendar.

I am therefore presenting the ancient Egyptian religious year as it might have been practiced in those very ancient times, when cultures such as those described in *The Bull of Ombos* were the norm. That is to say before the unification of Egypt circa 3100BCE, and before the hegemony of the cult of Horus and Osiris. This time before was one of strange, perhaps savage gods such as Seth. I think such a reconstruction is valuable, because the old ways had something of value that was lost in later, more civic orientated times. It can psychically refreshing to occasionally return to those times, and for those who practice magick, I'd say even more so.

THE LUNAR CALENDAR

The evidence for the old lunar calendar in Egypt is very complex. In the words of Leo Depuydt, it does not exactly jump out at you, whereas the existence of the well known Egyptian civil calendar, on which our own modern 365 day year derives, is beyond doubt. Alongside the well known civil calendar discussed elsewhere, several other calendars continued a parallel if more veiled existence. There is strong evidence for a 'secret' lunar calendar, in restricted use by the priesthood to determine the dates of one or two festivals, which unlike most others, really could not ignore their lunar roots. The *wag* festival of Thoth the moon god is one of those.

The best evidence for priestly use of a lunar calendar comes from records at Illahun or El Lahun, situated where the Bahr Yusuf canal enters the Fayum depression. The place is famous for the Kahun Papyri, many hundred of Hieratic texts, mathematical, medical, veterinary, and administrative documents. Among them, are the shift rosters for the cohorts of priests who staffed the Fayum's many temples. Egypt had very few permanent priests – most eligible men (and some women)[1] served the temple in rotation. A priest's tour of duty was always measured in lunar months.

In 1872, Heinrich Brugsch, published the first known example of a double date. ie an event dated in the 365 day year as well as the older lunar calendar. In the famous battle of Megiddo, Thutmose III waged war against the Syro-Palestinian city of Qadesh:

> In year 23 (of the reign of Thutmosis III), (civil day) I Shemu 21 (21st day of the first month of the harvest season), the day of the feast of Pesedjenet exactly (i.e: New Moon Day).[2]

There are about eight similar examples of where a day in the Egyptian civil calendar is supplemented by a reference to a lunar

---

1. Shaw, Ian (1995) *Dictionary of Ancient Egypt*, BM. 'priest'
2. Parker R (1950 : 29) *The Calendars of Ancient Egypt*, Chicago; Depuytd, L (1997) *Civil Calendar and Lunar Calendar in Ancient Egypt*, Leuven; for analysis of all available double dates. See also Faulkner (1942) 'The Battle of Megiddo' JEA XXVIII, 4, 11.

event – thus implying that another lunar calendar was in operation 'behind the scenes'.

It might be that the use of the lunar calendar was so familiar, that it was hardly ever written down. The Egyptians had names for each month – for example 'Mesore' (IV Shemu) but these rarely occur in inscriptions. Every native Egyptian just knew the name in the same way we know that 1/1 is 1st of January.[3]

The eight known double dates (more if you include other more ambiguous examples) probably refer to days of special importance in the month. These are, as listed in the temple rosters of Illahun:

Day 1	new moon	(*pesedenetew*)
Day 2	first crescent	(*tep 3bed*)
Day 4	Going forth of Sem priests	(*peret sem*)

---

3. The following is a rare example from the Almanac of Lucky & Unlucky Days that does list the seasonal month names alongside their individual names:
   I. akhet : Hours of Daylight, 16 Hours of Darkness, 8
   II. akhet: „ „   14   „ „   10 Phaophi.
   III akhet: „ „   12   „ „   12 Athyr.
   IV. akhet: „ „   10   „ „   14 Khoiak.
   I. peret: „ „   8   „ „   16 Tybi.
   II. peret: „ „   6   „ „   18 Mekhir.
   III. peret: „ „   8   „ „   16 Phamenoth.
   IV. peret: " "   10   " "   14 Pharmuthi.
   I. shomu: „ „   12   „ „   12 Pakhons.
   II shomu: „ „   12 (sic.) „ „ (blank) Payni
   III. shomu: „ „   16   „ „   8 Epeiph.
   IV. shomu: (blank) 18   „ „   6 Wp-mpt

Day 6   sixth day feast   (*senewet*)
Day 15 full moon   (*semedet*)

Other days mentioned elsewhere are:

Day 5   offerings on the altar (*jehet her hawet*)
Day 16 second arrival   (*meseper senenew*)
Day 23 second quarter day   (*denejet senenew*)

Dates such as the above form part of a lunar year that shadowed the civil year, and was therefore only of secondary importance. This is similar to the manner in which our own observations of the moon are less important than the familiar Gregorian calendar. The priests of Illahun were not addicted to moon watching. Like everyone else their focus was mainly on the civil calendar. A single priest, the so-called 'overseer of the hour' (*imeyew wenwet*)[4] was attached to each temple's House of Life. It was his job to say when the new 'temple' month should start. This he did by observation of the waning moon. Each night he looked for it in the sky. When it was invisible, day one of the cycle began in the morning. The lunar month had no special name but was simply (and for us confusingly) named after the civil month in which it started.

---

4. Well R A (1994) 'Re & the Calendars' in Spalinger (1994) *Revolutions in Time: Studies in Ancient Egyptian Calendars.*
5. Depuydt 1997 : 208

Sirius & the Lunar-Stellar Calendar

So far the discussion has been about a lunar calendar, clearly subordinated to the ancient Egyptian civil based year of 365 days. Now, I want to turn to the Sirius based system, whose existence has gradually emerged in the work of several scholars.[5]

The great pioneer in this field was Heinrich Brugsch, closely followed by Ludwig Borchardt. Their work was brought to a wider audience by Richard Parker, a professor at Brown University, Rhode Island, who wrote in English. All three men focused on a tiny informal calendar written on back of the beginning of a medical manuscript – the so-called Papyrus Ebers.

The Papyrus Ebers was bought from an Arab dealer in Luxor by Egyptologist George Ebers (1837-1898). It contains over a hundred columns of prescriptions, covering around 45 different classes of disease. It is normally paired up with the *Edwin Smith Surgical Papyrus*.

Time has always been an important aspect of healing. Ancient medical systems use a great many herbs in their medicaments, and these are often to be gathered by what we nowadays call 'bio-dynamic' principles, that is to say by observation of the sun and moon. So for example the potency of fresh herbs is likely to be greater if they are picked by moonlight.

Medical calendars are therefore strongly lunar. It's extremely likely that medical practitioners were another group that relied upon a lunar calendar well after it was abandoned in other walks of life. And sure enough, the reverse side of the *Papyrus Ebers* contains a

		Table 5: Month names of medical Papyrus Ebers		
A	B	C	D	E
		Transliteration & possible meaning	Associated deity	
1	wp-rnpt	opener of the year	Ra	iii Shemu (harvest)
2	thy	Tekhy - cup 'feast of drunkenness		iv Shemu
3	mnht	menekhet	Min	i Akhet (inundation)
4	Hwt-hr	Hathor	Hathor	ii Akhet
5	k3 hr k3	ka hor ka 'joining of kas'	Sokar / Osiris	iii Akhet
6	šf bdt	Shef bedet 'swelling of emmer wheat'		iv Akhet
7	rkh wr	Rekh wer 'greater burning' ie: cold season		i Peret (planting)
8	rkh ndš	rekh nedjes 'lesser burning'		ii Peret
9	Rnwtt	Renenutet	Renenutet	iii Peret
10	Hnśw	Khonsu	Khonsu	iv Peret
11	Hnt-hty	Khenty-khety	Horus	i Shemu (harvest)
12	jpt hmt	Ipet hemet	Ipet	ii Shemu

The Lunar Calendar with details of month names from Medical Papyrus Ebers

little calendar with huge implications. I won't repear everything I set out in my book *The Ritual Year in Ancient Egypt*. But the table on the right is an interpretations of the Ebers lunar calendar. This is the essential key to Egyptian religion. Even if it is routinely ignored in what are otherwise quite reasonable sources.

The Lunar month

The ancient Egyptian day began at dawn.[6] Contrast this with say the Jewish calendar where the day begins at sunset. The day and lunar month begin at the same time. The way they determined the first day of the month differs from many other ancient cultures with two notable exceptions – the Massai & the Loango of East Africa. The similarities may indicate Egyptian influence or perhaps African influence on ancient Egypt.

It is now widely accepted that the first day began on the morning after the final disappearance of the old crescent, i.e. when it is no longer visible in the eastern sky before sunrise.[7] This is an observation that requires no special skill and is as valid now as it was during ancient times. The only requirement being that you miss a few nights sleep during the final days of the waning moon. Now you might be saying to yourself "I can just look that up in an ephemeris or read it in the newspapers". All this is true, but it is good to remind yourself that the conjunction is an *invisible* event known nowadays by inference. It is not such a bad idea to consider

---

6. Our own term 'day' signifies a single unit of night and day; although actually our modern day begins at midnight. The word is thus a survival from older times when the day did literally begin at dawn or with the new day.
7. Parker (1950) Chapter 1

Hierogylphs of the dwat of early morning twilight

how you would determine this without all the conveniences of modern life. The observer needs to watch the moon carefully each night as it wanes digit by digit. If the crescent is no longer visible during a particular evening, when the sun rises it will be the first day of a new lunar month.

Almost all cultures have a name or symbol for this day. In the language of the ancient Egyptians, it is known as *pesedenet* (new moon). The names of the other thirty days of the month were first identified by Heinrich Brugsch in his 1883 Thesaurus.[8] We have already encountered some of these names in our earlier discussion on double dates (see above).

Some useful definitions for understanding Lunar calendars

As you probably know, when the sun and moon line up in the same part of the sky (ecliptic) it is known in astronomy as a conjunction, or in plain English as the new moon. Lunar calendars are always based on the period between one conjunction and the next, the so-called 'synodic' month. Because the moon has an elliptical orbit – it changes speed depending on its proximity to

---

8. Brugsch, Heinrich (1883) *Thesaurus Inscriptionum Aegyptiacarum*, 6 vols Leipzig. : 46-48.

the earth – the synodic month varies between 29.26 and 29.80 days.

The visibility of the old and new crescent varies in proportion to its latitude and 'anomaly' – in other words it is easier to see the crescent at Babylon than it is at Stonehenge.

If it weren't for these irregularities, then each lunar month would alternate between 29 and 30 days. However, in the real world it is quite possible to have several 30 day synodic months in succession. In addition to these natural 'irregularities' the observation of lunar cycles is subject to 'observer error'. For one reason or another, the old and new crescent may be unobserved or occulted by clouds.

For reasons such as the above, the apparent motion can be quicker in the first half of the month than it is in the second. Therefore, the half month also varies between 13.73 and 15.80 days.

The First Month of the Lunar Year

In the previous section, we discussed how to set the first day of the month. Now we must contsider how to determine the first lunar month of the yearly cycle. How does it all begin?

So far in this book, I have referred to an original lunar calendar existing before the Egyptian dynasties. This was a thesis first advanced by Richard Parker in his groundbreaking monograph

---

9. Parker (1950)
10. Wells, RA 1994 'Re and the Calendars' in Spalinger (1994) (ed.) in *Revolutions in Time: Studies in Ancient Egyptian Calendars*, Van Siclen, Texas.

*The Calendars of Ancient Egypt.*⁹ Recent research has refined this view, and identified that there were in fact at least two lunar calendars operating in pre-dynastic Egypt – one based in the north and the other in the south.¹⁰

The Southern version, centred around the predynastic culture of Nagada, was regulated by the Heliacal rising of Sirius, which, six thousand or so years ago occurred close to the Summer Solstice. The northern version, centred around Heliopolis, was regulated by the 'Birth of Ra' at the winter solstice.

The Northern Lunar-Solar Winter Solstice Version

In the north, in Egypt's Nile delta region, observations would probably have focussed on the Sun god's apparent 'journey' south and his eventual return. The journey is quite subtle, and involves observations of variations of the point at which the sun breaks over the horizon at dawn. It is the kind of observation that might be facilitated by structures such as the familiar stone and wooden henges of Neolithic Europe.

A number of Egyptian temples have winter solstice orientations, one of the best examples being the temple of Hatshepsut at Deir el Bahri. Very few temples have summer solstice orientation.

Observations are easier if several attendant stars point to and herald the principal star marker. So for example, Sothis, is 'heralded' by several stars in the Orion constellation – the triangle being: Betelgeuse, Rigel and then Sirius. These kind of observations are very like those described earlier in connection with the use of the moon's last crescent to determine the first day of the lunar month. A great many important events in ancient Egypt were determined by observations of the heliacal rising of stars and planets.

The sun god Ra's astronomical journey is mirrored in Egyptian mythology. He is born at the winter solstice, and enters the underworld – the *duat* at the vernal equinox. During the hours of 'night' he continues to travel and gestate there for the nine months (272 days) until, the following winter solstice, when he is again reborn. This mythology was underpinned by observations of the night sky, and especially the Milky Way. The Egyptians viewed the Milky Way as the body of the star goddess Nuit.

Richard Wells made the following interesting observation:

> 'It so happens that the outer arm of our galaxy, a band of myriads of stars called the Milky Way, when seen in its entirety over the course of a year has the appearance of a female shrouded in the thinnest of gauze robes (see illustration). The Milky Way bifurcates into two appendages at the constellation of Cygnus forming the legs of the anthropomorphic body. Further along, the star clouds swell in the vicinity of Gemini to form the head with even the suggestion of the cloth headdress, hanging down the back.'[11]

---

11. Wells, RA (1994) 'Re and the Calendars' in Spalinger, A J (1994) (ed.) in *Revolutions in Time: Studies in Ancient Egyptian Calendars*, Van Siclen, Texas.: 10

Ra enters the *duat* at sunset on the spring equinox. In terms of the cycle of the year, this could be considered as the god's conception. We can assume that our Egyptian ancestors marked the exact point at which the sun set on the horizon, by using a convenient landmark. If you were to look to that point in the west, an hour or two after sunset, when the sky is dark enough for you to see the Milky Way, you might observe an interesting phenomenon. The part of the Milky Way above identified as the head and especially the 'mouth' of Nuit, is over precisely the same spot. It is as if Nuit has just eaten the sun, which is in fact how this mystery is expressed in Egyptian mythology. The Birth of Ra occurs 272 days after conception on the morning of the winter solstice. This period of gestation is the same for us lesser mortals.

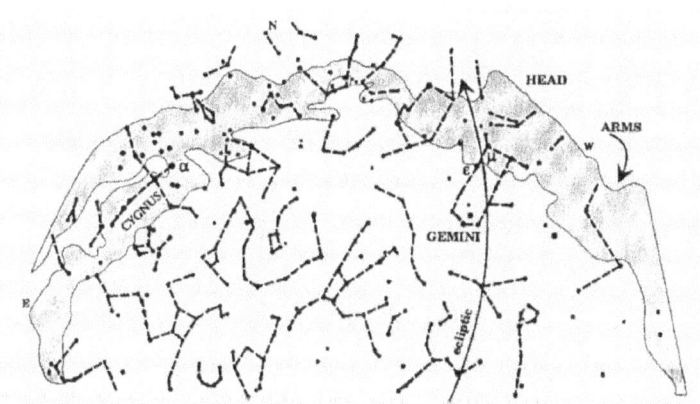

The stars of the Milky Way and their relationship to the star goddess Nwt.

Rather amazingly the Birth of Ra also has a stellar component. The winter sun rises against a backdrop of the constellation Cygnus, whose star 'Y' corresponds with the 'yoni' or womb of Nwt.

The attentive reader will have noticed that northern and southern calendars each have conflicting start dates. The ancient Egyptians tried to syncretise both calendars, which is another possible explanation for a 'problems' in later Egyptian month names eg: that *Mesore* which means 'Birth of Re' is the twelfth month of the year, when its name implies a beginning and therefore it should be the first month.

The South Lunar-Stellar or Lunar-Sothic Calendar Summer solstice (preferred)

This is my preferred version and the one I use as the basis for the Demonic calendar. The genesis of this Lunar-Sothic calendar is estimated to be 5000-4500BCE. Its use centred around the predynastic culture of Nagada. It was then that the heliacal rising of Sirius and the Nile flood would be historically closest.

Assumption: When records first began, the Nile flood and the heliacal rising of Sirius occurred close to the summer solstice. For the purpose of this calendar, the key observation remains the summer solstice.

Table 6: Ancient Egyptian Lunar Days - Light Half			
Lunar phase	Egyptian name (vocalic 'e' added for ease of reading)	Translation	Notes
1	*pešedeteyw*		
2	*tep 3bed*	new crescent day	
3	*mešeper*	arrival day	
4	*prt šem*	day of going forth of the Sem priest	
5	*3het h̭3t*	day of offerings on the altar	
6	*šenet*	sixth day	
7	*den3t*	part day, first quarter day	
8	*tep*		
9	*k3p*		
10	*šif*		
11	*šetet*		
12			
13	*m33 šty*		
14	*šl3w*		
15	*šemedet*	half-moon day, full moon	

Table 6: Names of the Lunar Days (from Heinrich Brugsch's Thesaurus Inscriptionum Aegyptiacarum*)*

Table 6: Ancient Egyptian Lunar Days - Light Half			
Lunar day	Egyptian name (vocalic 'e' added for ease of reading)	Translation	Notes
16	mešeper šen-new	second arrival day	
17	šȝw		
18	iʿh	day of the moon	
19	šedem medew.ef		
20	šetep		
21	ʿperew		
22	ph ʿsepedet		
23	denit	part day, last quarter day	
24	kenehw		
25	šetet		
26	peret		
27	wšb		
28	heb-šed newet	day of the going forth of Nuit	
29	ʿhȝ		
30	peret Min	day of the going forth of Min	

That southern or Upper Egypt was the locus for the Sirius based lunar calendar is underlined by the presence of a cult of Sirius at Egypt's frontier settlement at Elephantine. Elephantine, situated at the first cataract of the Nile, was considered to be the place where the Nile was born. This important regional centre has a ritual complex with a newly discovered shrine of the goddess Satet – the personification of Sirius.[12] The goddess Satet was identified with Sothis for at least 3000 years up to the Ptolemaic Greek era. The Sirius orientation is present in one of the doorways to the principal room of this shrine.

Every star has one conjunction with the sun every year. During this time, they are invisible to the earthly observer. This period of invisibility depends on the distance from the ecliptic, but for Sirius, the brightest of stars, its period of invisibility is approximately 70 days.

According to our Julian-Gregorian calendar, the Heliacal Rising of Sirius is set to around 17/19th July. As is well known, July is also the month of the annual Nile inundation, although like any natural phenomena, it is sometimes a day or two early or late, and sometimes it fails altogether. Actually These days Sirius rises in late August. These irregularities make it unlikely that it was the origin of a 365 day year.[13]

---

12. Wells 1986 *SAK*, 12 274 -275.

13. Nilsson uses the term 'pars pro toto' – the part stands for the whole this kind of observation

Theoretically the heliacal rising of Sirius should occur near to the first day of the first month of the year. However, because the Egyptians allowed their civil year to 'wander' both dates rarely coincided. Those occasions when they did was often utilized for some calendar reform. For example the introduction of the Julian calendar into Egypt, occurred at a time when the heliacal rising of Sirius, and the month I Akhet were in syncronisation.[14]

The heliacal rising of Sirius was known to the ancient Egyptians as *peret sepedet* – 'the going forth of Sothis', which was synonymous in later times with the phrase *wep renpet* – 'the opener of the year'. You have to ask yourself how the people of ancient Nagada co-ordinated the rising of this star with the waxing and waning of the moon? For example, did their lunar year begin the morning immediately following the heliacal rising? Or did the year start on the next new moon after its rising?

Here's the problem, what happens if there was still several days of the old lunar year still to go? In practice, the difference could be anything short of an entire lunar month. In other words, what happened if the moon was a clear but still waning crescent in the night sky?

The solution to this issue was probably as follows:

The lunar year began with the first new moon immediate after the heliacal rising of Sothis.

14. Depuydt (1997: 17)

Gods of Lunar Year					
Month	Neter	Name	Hieroglyph	
(Jul)	Thoth	Thoth	*dḥwty*	
1 (Jul-Aug)	Seth	Tekhy	*tḥy*	Akhet (inundation)
2 (Aug - Sep)	Min	Phaophi	*p n jpt*	
3 (Sep - Oct)	Hathor	Athyr	*Ḥwt-ḥr*	
4 (Oct-Nov)	Sokar	Choiak	*k3 ḥr k3*	
5 (Nov - Dec)	Neith	Tyby	*t3 ʿbt*	Peret (planting)
6 (Dec - Jan)	Nuit	Mechir	*mḥyr*	
7 (Jan-Feb)	Anubis	Pharmenoth	*p n jmn ḥtp*	
8 (Feb - Mar)	Renenutet	Pharmuthi	*p n rnwtt*	
9 (Mar - Apr)	Khonsu	Pachon	*Ḥnśw*	Shemu (harvest)
10 (Apr -	Horus	Payni	*Ḥnt-ḥty*	
11 (May -	Ipet	Epiphi	*ʿIpt*	
12 (Jun - Jul)	Ra	Mesore	*mswt rʿ*	

An extra or intercalary or epagomenal month of Thoth is added to the lunar calendar every two to three years to keep it synchronized with the seasons.

You might want to refresh your memory with the section above on how to determine a new moon. Now this bit is tricky. If the new moon occurs within less than 11 days of the heliacal rising of Sirius there needs to be an intercalary or thirteenth lunar month added to the year to correct things. Scholars think this extra inserted month, occurring approximately every three years, and was dedicated to Thoth.[15]

The naming of Egyptian months can sometimes be confusing, precisely because of this ambiguity. In the lunar calendars known of from other cultures, intercalary or straddle months have no unique name, but merely repeat the name of either the last or occasional the first month of the year. For example, speaking of the Jewish calendar, which is still lunar, there is the account of Gamaliel II, one of the three learned Rabbi's charged with the task of keeping the calendar in tune with the seasons. He writes:[16]

---

15. See thirteen moons of the North American tradition. Cycle starts again with new moon after winter solstice - if extra needed use Ice moon, otherwise its: Long Night; Ice; Snow; Death; Awakening; Grass; Planting; Rose; Lightning; Harvest; Hunter's; Falling Leaf & Tree.

    Ever wondered why it is traditional for some to celebrate the 12 days of Christmas? 11 is the number of days difference between the lunar and solar years.

16. Quoted in M. Nilsson *Primitive Time Reckoning* (1920 : 245). He writes that the ancient Hebrews adopted the 'Canaanite' versions of month names. Given their history one might assume they knew those of Egyptian but chose not to use them apart from shared words such as Yahel – 'Full Moon'.

'We make known to you that the lambs are small and the young of the birds are tender and the time of the corn harvest has not come, so that it seems right to me and my brothers to add to this year thirty days.'

It seems likely that the Egyptians had a similar system, repeating one of their month names where needed, approximately every three years. Thus, the straddle month has various names including: *wep renpet* : 'opener of the year' and Ra Horakhty: 'Horus of the two horizons'. In the original lunar-stellar calendar, the first fixed month 'Tekhen' was an Egyptian New Year feast of 'drunkenness'. Whoever invented the later festival calendar, replaced Tekhen with the name Djhuty or Thoth. There is a theory that Thoth's name had previously been reserved for the occasional extra or intercalary thirteenth lunar month that was to be added to the cycle every third year.

In the archaic lunar calendar, the subsequent months were then named after whichever god's feast actually fell in that month. The mortuary temple of Rameses II (1279-1213BCE) has what is usually considered to be a technically superior version of the lunar calendar.[17]

The Babylonian lunar calendar avoided 'leap years' by using a nineteen year cycle which, plotted all 235 lunations over the period

---

17. See Parker (1950 : 42) – In the first column of the Ebers calendar the last month of the year appears at the head of the months merely because its eponymous feast determined the following year.

– 12 years of 12 lunar months, interspersed with 7 years of 13 lunar months. It is possible that the Egyptians considered something similar in the Carlsberg Papyrus but its speculations were unlikely to have ever been used.

The Demonic Calendar

THE DECANS

"The snake is in my hand and cannot bite me" [1]

"Oh lion and serpent who destroys the destroyer, be mighty among us" [2]

WHAT IS A DEMON?

The Egyptians, like many cultures, had no generic word for "demon". Etymologically, the Greek derived term "daemon" or "demon" means divider or alloter, and from Homer's time onwards, an operator of unexpected & intrusive events in a person's life. Unlike Olympian gods, daemon was an impersonal thing, unpredictable, anonymous & often frightful in manifestation. Thus connected with fate. (Oxford Dictionary of the Classical World). Plato, perhaps influenced by Egyptian and Hindu thought, added a new concept of the "guardian daemon" that accompanied a person in life, & postmortem, acted as one's judge or advocate. Contemporary magical practitioners often describe a spiritual entity known as the Holy Guardian Angel, that is attached or comes into existence at birth or conception.

The ancient Egyptians did recognise three categories of sentient beings: The Ankhew, the Akhew and the Neterew which can be translated as the Living, the Dead and the Gods. All three have their good and bad sides.

---

1. Coffin Text 885 ancient words to ward off evil, quoted in Ritner (1993)
2. Aleister Crowley (1973) "Gnostic Mass" in *Magick: Liber ABA*, Routledge

There is quite a lot of information to be had concerning the ancient Egyptian fear of attack from night demons. But, because of a general prejudice amongst old guard Egyptologists, much of this information is buried in obscure academic publications.

Spells, such as the following lay untranslated for years after its discovery, until in 1990 Robert Ritner, an expert of Ancient Egyptian magick, took another look. To paraphrase his translation:

Oh male adversary (*ḏ3y*),
Oh female adversary,
Oh male ghost,
Oh female ghost
Oh dead men,
Oh dead women,
be far from me.
Listen but do not come.
your faces are twisted backwards
your limbs are unsound.
Your heart is destined for the sacrificial meal
of the Cobra Goddess.
NN born of NN has extracted your hearts,
Oh dead ones.
He has taken your hearts,
Oh dead men and dead women.
You shall be eaten by the Cobra Goddess
and shall not live
Your limbs are offering cakes.
You will not escape the four noble ladies
You will not escape the fortress of Horus Imy Senwet [6]

THE DREAMY NIGHT AIR

The spell reveals the way most Egyptians viewed the perils of the night. These entities can be dangerous, and there is a relationship between them and certain kinds of illness. Central to the process are night demons, 'vampiric' entities that are known to us now as *incubi* or *succubi*. These creatures attack sexually, entering the body of their victims, perhaps during lovemaking, taking sexual and other body fluids such as blood.

And neither are Egyptian demons a completely separate species. They come from the same familiar categories mentioned above, the living, the dead or the gods. Egyptian demons can be minor deities bullied into doing unpleasant tasks by the big gods. It is possible that this category of god/demon was particularly fearful to the ordinary folk who were often afraid of the gods who lived in the temple. But broadly speaking the demons fall into two broad camps.

i. Those that are emanations of the well known gods and goddesses of Egypt.
ii. Those that are related to the world of men.

Of those related to the gods one of the most common is the moon god Khonsu. Almost as common are those related to the goddess Hathor in the form of the so-called Seven Hathors. The Hayety (*ḥȝy.ty*) demon was the emissary of Hathor or the Shemay (*šmȝ.y*) demon, emissary of Bastet. For most Ancient Egyptians the world of the emissaries was far more real and immediate than that of the abstract gods whose cult was kept alive by the temple priests. These entities were widely feared throughout Egypt. Left to their own devices they could determines a person's fate at birth, when it was written down in Hathor's *Great Book of*

Fate. When the time came, Hathor sent out her emissaries or 'flower cutters' to reap that day's harvest of souls:

> 'Then the seven Hathors came to see her and said with one voice "It is by the ('executioner's) blade that she shall die" ' – *Tale of Two Brothers*

> 'Presently the Hathors came to determine a fate for him and said "He shall die through a crocodile, or a snake or even a dog".' – *Tale of the Doomed Prince*

Another great category of demon were spirits of place, heaven, earth but especially water.

THE DEMONIC CALENDAR

The demonic calendar is based on the decans. I'm not sure anyone has previously called these personifications of the decans, demons, but that is what they plainly are. To use the title of a recent groundbreaking academic conference, these are "demon things" and there are actually far more images of them in ancient Egyptian iconography than there are the well known deities.

The ancient Egyptians divided the year into 36 weeks of ten days duration, hence "decan" from Greek "ten". The *Book of Nwt* tells us of the God Shu, who personifies the wind, air and atmosphere. It is Shu who controls the ebb and flow of the decans. When the stars are visible at night the Egyptians saw them as metaphorically *outside* the body of Nwt. Thus when the stars are visible they are in the realm of Shu, who uses the four winds to direct their movement. Some images of Nwt show her surrounded by images of the four winds. The iconography of the decans predates that of all famous European books of magick such as the

Testament of Solomon or the *Goetia*. But one thing all these spirits have in common is their malign character.

In Egypt, as in many other places, the lunar month lasted approximately 30 days, and could therefore be divided into three trimesters, each of ten days, which is a decan or Egyptian 'week'. Therefore the entire year had 36 weeks or decans. Each decan is ruled over by particular stars, rising in sucession over the course of a year. These can be observed rising on the eastern horizon just before dawn. This star changes position or rises by approximately one degree each day. After ten days a new decanal star makes its appearance. The old star continues to rise through the year, culminating in the "middle of the sky" (midheaven) then declining again to the west before disappearing from view.

Moving at the rate of one degree a day it takes about eight weeks to ascend to the middle of the sky. It will remain visible there for a further twelve weeks. Its final nine weeks will be descending slowly to the west before spending seven weeks in the "Underworld" and invisible to us.

You and I were born into this intricate web of stars. The 36 decans are in effect an earlier Egyptian equivalent of the later Greek system of twelve zodiacal signs. The twelve *culminating* decans are also the equivalent of the twelve "houses".

There is a *Book of Nwt* which is, in effect, a snapshot of the sky at one particular moment in time. The book was found inscribed on a monument that dates from the time of Sety I of the 19th dynasty (circa 1350BCE). But it is actually a picture of the sky from an earlier time, it show the position of the stars when Egypt was first unified around 3300BCE! Some of the hieroglyphs drawn within the body of Nwt show an even older

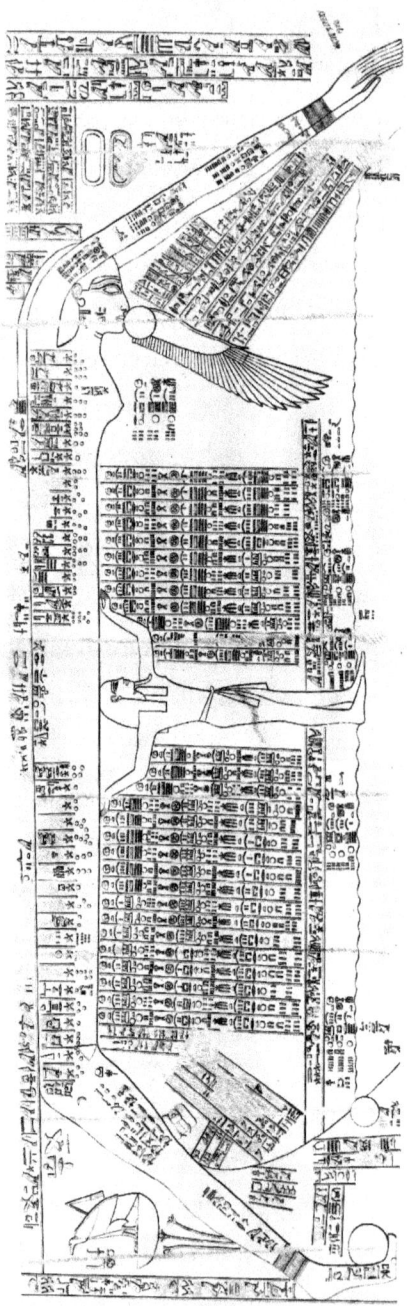

Astrological ceiling from roof of sarcophagus chamber, the Osireion, Abydos (Published by H Frankfort, from a tracing made by W.B. Emery).
Width 10.25meters. Orientation N-S

sky. These particular moments in time were obviously of special importance and they recur on Egyptian monuments again and again.

The very famous circular astronomical ceilings from Dendara, in particular what's known as Dendera B which is now in the Louvre, uses the native system of decans, as well as the Greco-Babylonian signs of the zodiac. The Egyptian decans were eventually absorbed into the Greek system. The Egyptians accepted many new Babylonian and Greek astrological

ideas. But in the case of the 36 decans they could insist on the priority of their own native system. The decans continue to be an important aspect of tropical astrology, its Egyptian legacy.

In Egyptian star-lore, "horoscopes" tend to document the negatives present at a person's birth. This use of astrology is similar to later "tantrik" attitudes. This is knowledge that might be helpful to *decondition* oneself and to *avoid* fate. It is about wiping one's name from that great *Book of Fate*. There is another group of demons, known as the Hateyew (ḥ3tyw) who are the emissaries of Shu or of Hathor. Their function is to reap a sinister harvest of humanity. They act on the basis of these "reports" or records in the Book (of Calamities). So best to know what is in that book and if possible erase the entry! [3]

THE STAR GODDESS

Aleister Crowley's evocation of Nuit, Nwt (or Newet) in *Liber AL* [4] focuses our attention on a very unusual and unique Egyptian Goddess. The sky Goddess Nwt is one of the oldest deities in the Egyptian pantheon. Her first appearance in prehistory was as a clan deity. The really old Goddesses often had a bovine form. Thus Nwt is described in *Pyramid Text* spell 548 as a long horned celestial cow who suckles the king and takes him to

---

3. See A S von Bomhard *(2008) The Noas of the Decans*, Oxford

4. Notes for short presentation at Treadwell's, April 9th 2012. Feast for the reception of the *Book of the Law*, organised by Entelechy, Greece. Main sources consulted Morgan, M, *Wheel of the Year in Ancient Egypt* (Mandrake) for transcription of the "Book of Nuit" ritual drama, linked to one of thirteen lunar feasts of the archaic ritual year. Hollis, Susan T "Women of Ancient Egypt and the sky Goddess Nut" *Journal of American Folklore* 100 (1987). Hollis, Susan T "Five Egyptian Goddesses in the third millennium BC" KMT 5,4 (1994) 48-49; Lesko, Barbara (1999) S *The Great Goddesses of Egypt*;

herself in the sky: "May Nwt the Great put her hands on him/ she the long of horn, the pendulous of breast". Over time she assume human form.

In many mythologies the sky is a God, i.e. male and its counterpart is the Great Earth Mother. The Egyptian personification of the sky as female is unique.

Her name literally means "The watery one" (Nw.t). She represents "the sky" but not as a lifeless roof of heaven but as a dynamic entity, creating and destroying. She also represented the entire sky, night and day as well as large features such as the Milky Way. [5]

The largest representations of Nwt, indeed any deity in Egypt are to be found in the first hypostyle hall of the temple of Hathor at Dendara. Dendara is the main cult centre of the Cow Goddess Hathor. Nwt's appearance at Dendara underlines the fact that she has no exclusive cult centre in her own right. She is invariably worshipped in a small chapel in association with another God or Goddess. This does not detract from her status but is the natural consequence of her universal, otherworld role.

As time went by Nwt become part of the so-called mortuary cult in which she is the personification of the coffin. The coffin can be viewed as a stylised *womb*. Wrapped inside this womb, the deceased waits to be reborn after a long period of incubation.

---

5. see Hollis 1994: 87
6. From a New Kingdom coffin in tomb of Hattiay at Thebes, the singer of Amon henut-wadjebu now in Cleveland Museum of Art No 61

"Oh my mother Nwt, stretch yourself over me, that I may be placed amongst the imperishable stars, which are in you, and that I may not die." [6]

The female sky is the realm of the dead, whereas the Earth is for the living. This perhaps explains the male rulership of the Earth. In other cultures the movement of time and space was a role ascribed to male deities such as Marduk, Yahweh, or Mithras. In ancient times before the patriarchal religions, great Goddesses may well have taken a more central role in this.

Top register of gatehouse at Medinet Habu, the exacrated figure is Seth, the accompanying inscription says the figure left of Seth is the Goddess Nwt.

One important aspect of Nwt, especially in Ramesside times is a connection with the God Seth. One of his most important epithets is "Son of Nwt". Now of course as mother of all the Gods this epithet could be taken by any. Even so it seems to be especially associated with Seth. Seth was often depicted in the presence of Nwt, for instance at the memorial chapel of Ramesses III at Medinat Habu. The 72 Companions of Seth are stars in her body, he leads them in a diurnal dance around the celestial pole. These 72 stars are synonymous with the decans.

THE BOOK OF NWT

Nwt is intimately connected with the stars, especially those that are close to and appear to envelop our world. You may be familiar with the following image of Nwt at the moment of creation:

It shows a key moment in the unfolding of the cosmos as envisaged by the priests of Heliopolis. Just to remind you, in this system, creation

---

7. His famous act of autoerotic creation encapsulates male and female motifs - masturbation/ejaculation (male) swallowing/birthing (female)

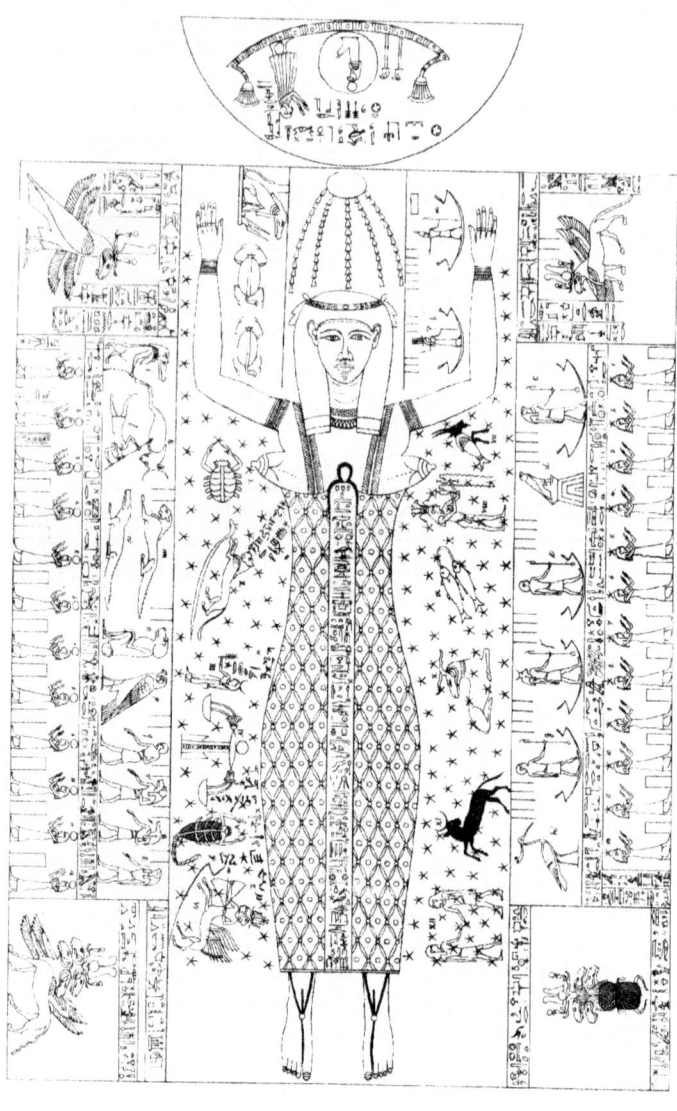

Coffin of Heter, from Neugebauer O & Parker, R (1962) *Ancient Egyptian Astronomical Texts*, 4 vols, Brown University. Now lost published by H Brugsch, *Recueil de monuments égyptiens dessinés sur lieux et publ. par H. Brugsch. [With] Geographische Inschriften altägyptischer Denkmäler, von J. Duemichen. 6 pt. [in 7]*.

begins with the ambisexual [7] Amun-Ra or Sungod Ra. He has the power to emanate parts of himself, creating other Gods and Goddesses. He starts with Shu and Tefnut, who represent the principles of air and fire respectively. The process of emanation continues and they generate Nwt the sky Goddess and Geb the Earth. Initially Nwt and Geb are locked together in a sexual embrace, almost a single entity. It is Shu, the God of the winds and the air who separates them, creating a space between all these elements in which our world can exist.

Look again at the image of Nwt in on page 36. You see the elongated body of Nwt, Geb (the floor) and Shu in the centre separating them. To the untrained eye a jumble of hieroglyphs are written all over the picture. This text was originally known to Egyptologists as *The Book of Nwt*. More recent research has uncovered the original if slightly less elegant title the *Book of the Fundamentals of the Course of the Stars*.[8]

The texts to the left indicated by the image of a falcon with a flail, concern the rising Sun; those to the extreme right the setting Sun. The large collection of vertical hieroglyphic text between Nwt and Geb concerns the "decans" of the visible stars. The vertical lines of hieroglyphs *inside* the body of Nwt, is another, much older system of decans, perhaps obsolete or concerned with an even earlier lunar calendar.

---

8. Leitz (1995 3-57) quoted in A S von Bomhard (2008) *The Noas of the Decans*, Oxford

THE EGYPTIAN DECANS

The remainder of this book is a popular list of decans and their demons, along with their meanings where known. Despite a great deal of research to compile this list, there are still some gaps and anomalies, but it is an essential guide. You will still have to supplement this with data drawn from your own experience as well as updates and revisions from the websites connected with this book. If you look for me on Twitter you will find I post regular updates in real time.

To use this ephemeris you will to need to know the date in the standard calendar of the new moon immediately *after* the summer solstice. This data is published in most standard diaries. Earlier I explained how to calculate these dates for yourself, just in case you find yourself on a desert island. It can be used to calculate the cycle of decanal demons in the year to come. It can also be used to calculate the demon that was present at your birth or at other important moments in your life. This was the Egyptian equivalent of a horoscope. The so called triplicities in modern astrology are the Egyptian legacy to that arte. To calculate your birth demon you will need to know the dates of the new moons in the year of your birth. It is said that on your birthday, this demon is closest to you, and for some, this is a guardian daemon.

Here is example for 2020:
The summer solstice occurs on the 20th June.
The New Moon is one day later on 21st. June. The first lunar month of the year therefor begins on 21st June and others follow accordingly. The only other important consideration that matters is whether the coming lunar year has 12 or 13 months, remembering that all lunar calendars require an extra month every now and again.

If the new moon occurs within less than 11 days of the solstice there needs to be an intercalary or thirteenth lunar month added to the year to correct things. This extra inserted month, occurring approximately every three years, was dedicated to Thoth.

The new moon in 2020 does indeed occur within 11 days, the next day in fact so there must be an additional or Thoth month. In terms of the decanal sequence, the first three decans must be repeated.

Just to make that clear

21 Jun – 29th Jun	1st Decan – Sothis
30 Jun – 7th Jul	2nd Decan – Setew
08 Jul – 19th Jul	3rd Decan – Kenemet
20 Jul – 30th Jul	1st Decan (repeated) – Sothis
31 Jul – 09th Aug	2nd Decan (repeated) – Setew
10 Aug – 18th Aug	3rd Decan (repeated) – Kenmet
19 Aug – 28th Aug	4th Decan – Khery kheped kenmet
29 Aug – 7th Sep	5th Decan – Heset djat
08 Sep – 16th Sep	6th Decan – Phewy
17 Sep – 26 Sep	7th Decan – Temat heret kheret
and so on	

Lucky & Unlucky days

Depending on which version of the almanac one consults, the day is said to have either two or three parts. Thus the first column of the almanac has either the hieroglyph:

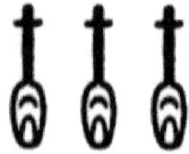

NFR, NFR, NFR -
(F)ORTUNATE, F. F.

or

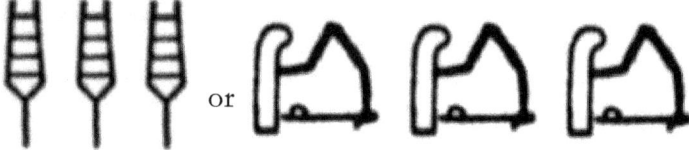

AHA, AHA, AHA (ꜥḥꜣ, ꜥḥꜣ, ꜥḥꜣ)
(A)DVERSE, A. A.

Hence some days can be one part favourable, two parts unfavourable. The ephemeris includes traditional events and prognosis each day. Some have used this, I'd say unreliably, as the basis of a modern reconstructed ritual calendar. Also called a calendar in some published translations, it is more of an almanac than a calendar. This explains why several well known feasts are actually missing

You may be wondering why some days were lucky and others unlucky. Modern computer aided analysis of the text has yield a interesting reason for this. The variations seem to follow the pulse cycle of the binary star Algol –

The first and last days of each month are always lucky, the only exception to this rule is II Peret (Harvest) 30.

The 20th day is invariably adverse.

The 10th day is always favourable in Akhet (Inundation); in the archaic lunar calendar to be discussed in a later chapter, the 10th would fall at the beginning of the 'white nights' of the moon's middle phase. This day is always adverse in Peret (Winter) and alternative adverse and favourable in Shemw (Harvest).

Almanac of Lucky & Unlucky Days

An introduction to the beginning of infinity and the end of eternity which the gods and goddesses of the shrine and the assembly of the Ennead have made (and) which the majesty of Thoth has gathered together in the great house in the presence of the Lord of the Universe. what has been found in the library in the rear-house of the Ennead.

House of Ra (Tomorrow)

House of Osiris (Yesterday)

House of Horus (Today)

		Decan	Page
Inundation	1 Akhet	1	49
		2	51
		3	53
	2 Akhet	4	56
		5	58
		6	60
	3 Akhet	7	62
		8	64
		9	66
	4 Akhet	10	68
		11	70
		12	72
Winter	1 Peret	13	74
		14	76
		15	78
	2 Peret	16	80
		17	82
		18	84
	3 Peret	19	86
		20	88
		21	90
	4 Peret	22	92
		23	94
		24	96
Summer	1 Shemu	25	98
		26	100
		27	102
	2 Shemu	28	104
		29	106
		30	108
	3 Shemu	31	110
		32	112
		33	114
	4 Shemu	34	116
		35	118
		36	120

Also see ephemeris for future years on page 138

(1st Decan)
Akhet Month I
Season of Inundation
1st Trimester (circa. July)[9]

Egyptian name:
Sothis (*sepedet*).

Image
Goddess Isis with feather crown

Mineral:
Gold or Lapis Lazuli

Abramelin:
Morech, Serep, Proxone, Nablum, Kosem,
Peresh, Thirana, Aluph, Neschamah, Milon,

Aspect:
DAY 1: F. F. F. The birth of Ra-Harakhte; ablution throughout the entire land in the water of the beginning of the High Nile which comes forth as fresh Nun, so they say. And so, all gods and goddesses are in great festivity on this day, and everybody likewise.

---

9. All the following correspondences are based on the so-called Sety I B family of decans as described in Neugebauer & Parker (1960) *Egyptian Astronomical Texts, vol III Decans, Constellations and Zodiacs*. The aspects are taken from *The Cairo Calendar* (1960) translation by Abd el-Mohsen Bakir (actually more of an Almanac than a calendar). See earlier discussion for the arrangement of Abramelin daemons. I've also added at the end the decans as listed in Budge, E.A. Wallis. *The Gods of the Egyptians, Or, Studies in Egyptian Mythology* (1904). He used various sources.

DAY 2: F. F. F. If you see anything [in the sky], it will be good on this day. It is the day of the going out of the Ennead before Ra, their hearts being pleased when they see his youthfulness (after) they had killed him who rebelled against their master, and overthrown *Apophis* wherever he might be who fell on his back amidst the flood.

DAY 3: F. F. A. Anyone born on this day will die by a crocodile. It is the day of making *ipy* in the river by (?) the gods of the Duat.

DAY 4: F. F. A. Do not do anything on it this day. It is the day of the going forth by Hathor together with the executioners (flowercutters) in order to approach the river-bank. Now the gods go in a contrary wind. Do not navigate in a boat on this day.

DAY 6: F. F. F. If you see anything, it will be good on this day (it will be good). The gods are peaceful in heaven at navigating the great barque.

DAY 6: A. A. F. Anyone born on this day will die of the trampling of a bull.

DAY 7: F. F. F. It is the day of welcoming the inundation and offering to the gods. If you see anything [in the sky], it will be good on this day.

DAY 8: F. F. A. Do not go out at night-time, because Ra goes forth ... As for him who navigates Nun, and as for anybody who is shipwrecked, on water make occasion on water on this day.

DAY 9: F. F. F. If you see anything, it will be good (on this day). It is (the day), of pacifying the heart of those who are in the-horizon in front of the Majesty of Ra.

DAY 10: F. F. F. It is the day of (the going forth of) Hedj-Hotpe (goddess of weaving) while-all gods and goddesses are in festivity. As, to anybody born on this day, he will die as an honoured one in (old age).

1. Ṭepā-Kenmut.

1. Ṭepā-Kenmut . .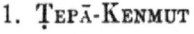

(2nd Decan)
Akhet Month I
Season of Inundation
2nd Trimester (circa. Jul - Aug)

Egyptian name:
Setew (*št(w)*)

Image:
Ibis or serpent headed God, standing, offering two nw-jars.

Mineral:
Carnelian and gold

Aspect:

DAY 11: A. A. A. Kindle fire on it (i.e. this day). It is the day of-the going forth of the great fire spitting cobra raging in the inaccessible shrine . . . Do not look at a bull, and do not make love on this day.

DAY 12: A. A. A. Do not go out on this day. Spend the day until Ra sets in his horizon. It is the day of the crew whom Ra separates from one another. As to anyone disobeying Ra, his house will fall down at once.

DAY 13: F. A. A. Anyone born on this day will die of blindness. It is the day of *Mrt-sm't* (musician goddess perhaps Neith's) massacre.

DAY 14: (NO SPACE) The day of the great Offering (*3ʿbt*) in the southern heaven (Orion) on this day. Offer to your city gods, for it is pleasant to the gods.

DAY 15: F. A. A. Do not proceed in a boat on this day. It is the day of the rage (in.) the Duat, one shall have no knowledge thereof. Lo, the rowers are on the river on this day. Do not ... (on) this day.

DAY 16: A. A. A. As to anyone born on this day he will die by a crocodile. It is the day of ...... by Neith.

DAY 17: A. A. A. Do not eat any *mehyet*-fish on this day. It is the day of (taking away) Sobek's offering on this day, namely, taking away the offering (from) his mouth on this day.

DAY 18: F. F. F. If you see anything it will be good on this day. It is the day of magnifying the Majesty of Horus more than his brother, which they *(i.e.* the gods) did at the portal.

DAY 19: F. F. F. A happy day in heaven in front of Ra, l. p. h.(life, prosperity and health) the great Ennead is in great festivity. (Burn) incense on the fire for his follower? (in) the Mesektet Mandjet and the gods. It is the day of receiving... It is the day of the going forth... the necropolis before Babai (red eared Baboon) ... his

DAY 20: A. A. A. Do not do any work. It is the day when the great ones followers of Horus and Seth are partial.

Abramelin:

Frasis, Haja, Malacha, Molabeda, Yparcha,

Nudatoni, Methaera, Bruahi, Apollyon, Schaluah,

2. Kenmut.

2. Kenmut . . . .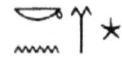

(3rd Decan)
Akhet Month I
Season of Inundation
3rd Trimester
(circa. August)

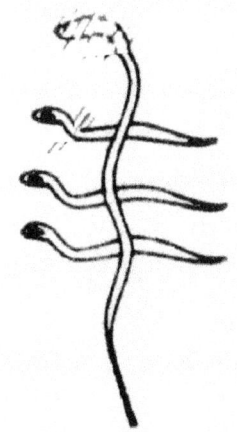

Egyptian name:
Kenemet (*knm(t)*) "Darkness"

Image:
Erect serpent with three smaller serpents

Mineral:
Garnet

Aspect:
Day 21: F. F. F. Take a holiday on this day; offer to the followers of Ra on this day. Do not kill a bull, and do not let (it) pass before your face (or even) buy it (i.e. the bull) from another one on this day. It is the day to be cautious of it.

Day 22: A. A. A. Ra calls every god and every goddess, and they await his arrival. He lets them enter into his belly. Then they began to move about within him; then he killed them all, then he vomited them into water. They turned into fish, and the souls became birds which flew to heaven. The bodies (became) fish, and the souls (Ba) into birds which are not caught (and) fish on ... as far as this day. Do not eat fish on this day. Do not warm oil; (do not eat) birds.

Day 23: A. A. A. Do not burn incense on fire for the god on this day. Do not kill any protective (*ʿnḥy*)- serpent (or) any creature among the birds. Do not eat it on this day. Do not listen to singing or dancing on this day. (It is the day of) causing the heart of the enemy of Ra l.p.h. (life, prosperity anf health) to suffer on account of what he has done against his children on this day. As to anyone born on this day he will not live.

DAY 24: F. F. F. The Majesty of this god sails with a favourable wind peacefully ... Behold, he settles down, his heart especially. Then he appeared in the Mesektet-boat, and (then) rising in the Mandjet-boat. As for anyone born on this day (he will die) as an honoured one in old age.

DAY 25: F. F. A. Do not go out of your house on any road at the time of (night). It is the day of the going out of Sekhmet to the eastern district, and of the repelling of the confederates of Seth. As for any lion whom they approach he will pass away at once.

DAY 26: A. A. A. Do not do anything on this day. It is the day of Horus fighting with Seth. Everyone embraced his fellow, and they were on their backs as two men. They were turned into ebony in the Duat... (They spent) three days and four nights in this manner. Then Isis let (a harpoon) down and (it fell) before her son, Horus. He then called with a loud voice saying: 'Behold, (I am her son, Horus).' Then Isis called on this harpoon saying: 'Loosen, loosen from (my) son, Horus.' Thereupon, this harpoon (loosened) from her son, Horus. Then she let down another harpoon which fell in front of Seth. Then he cried saying: 'Behold, I am her brother, Seth.' Then she called on this harpoon: 'Be strong, be strong.' Then this Seth called on her many times saying: 'Do you prefer the foreign man to an uncle?' Then she ... evil ... Then she called on this harpoon saying: 'Loosen, loosen. Behold, my brother of my mother.' Thereupon this harpoon turned away from him. Then they *stood* up as two men, and one turned his back on his fellow. Then the majesty of Horus became angry with his mother, Isis, like a panther. She stood before him...

DAY 27: F. F. F. Peace on the part of Horus with Seth. Do not kill any *protective (ꜥnḥy)*- serpent on this day; make a holiday.

DAY 28: F. F. F. The gods are happy on this day when they see (Horus & Seth) the children of Nut peaceful and content. If you see anything, it will be good on this day.

DAY 29: A. F. F. Do not kindle fire in the house on this day. Do not burn ointment; do not go out by night on this day.

(LAST DAY): F. F. F. If you see anything [in the sky], it will be good on this day.

Abramelin:

Myrmo, Melamo, Pother, Schad, Echdulon, Manmes, Obedomah, Iachil, Ivar, Moschel,

3. Kher-khept-Kenmut.

(4th Decan)
Akhet month II
season of inundation
1st trimester
(circa. august)

Egyptian name:

Khery kheped kenemet

(*ḥry ḥpd knm(t)*)

"Down there, darkness"

Image:

lion-headed Goddess, uraeus or disk on head, seated, scepter & ankh.

Mineral:

Glass and gold

Aspect:

DAY 1: F. F. F. Jubilation - The great Ennead is in festivity on this day. It is the day of establishing the heritage of the Great One.

DAY 2: ?.?.?. The proceeding of the Horus the Elder of Lower Egypt to his mother Neith to see that he was suffering from his buttocks (due to homosexual abuse). Repetition of birth ... great (festivity) in heaven. Offer to all gods. It is important to hear what I say to you.

DAY 3: F. F. F. Thoth in the presence of Ra in the inaccessible shrine. He gave the written order of the reconciliation of the Wedjat-eye; Hu and Sia were among (his) followers ..?.?.. in his manner. If you see anything [in the sky]. It will be good on this day.

DAY 4: A. F. A. Anyone born on this day will die of skin-rash. It is the day of the going forth of Anubis for the inspection of this wabet (*wʿbt*) for the protection of the body of the god.

DAY 5: A. A. A. Do not go out of your house on any road on this day. Do not copulate with a woman. It is the day of offering in the presence of the weaver god Hedj-hotpe (and) Montu on this day. Anyone born on this day will die (of) copulation.

DAY 6: F. F. F. A happy day for Ra in heaven, and the gods are pacified in his presence. The Ennead is making glorification in front of the Lord of the Universe. Anyone born on this day will die in a state of drunkenness.

DAY 7: A. A. A. Do not do anything on this day. The going of Ra ... to the countries which he has created in order to kill the children of Bedesh (Apophis) and the return of Ra on (this day)... his neck. Then he killed them before his Ennead. Anyone born on this day will die in foreign lands.

DAY 8: F. F. F. If you see anything on this day it will be good.

DAY 9: F. F. F. Jubilation in the heart of Ra ... His Ennead is in festivity, all enemies are overthrown on this day. Anyone born on this day will die at a good old age.

DAY 10: (F. F. F.). Proceeding of the Majesty of Bastet, mistress of Ankh-towe, and the inquiry of the Majesty of Ra in Heliopolis about her going to pay tribute to the holy tree (upon which royal names are inscribed). It is agreeable to the heart of his followers.

Abramelin:

Peekah, Hasperim, Kathim,
Porphora, Badet,
Kohen, Lurchi, Falfuna, Padidi,
Helali,

4. Ḥā-tchat.

4. Ḥā-TCHAT

(5th Decan)
Akhet Month II
SEASON OF INUNDATION
2nd Trimester (circa. Aug - Sep)

Egyptian name:

Heset djat (*hst ḏ3t*)

"Minister praise"

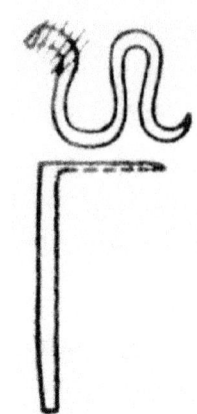

Image:

Serpent on a support

Mineral:

Glass and Gold

Aspect:

DAY 11: F. F. F. Fixing the front piece at the front of the prow of the barque on this day. Life and prosperity are before the holy tree. Which is established behind him. Everything is good on this day.

DAY 12: A. A. A. It is the day on which he who rebelled against his lord raised his head. His Utterance has annihilated the speech of Seth, son of Nut. The separation of his head is inflicted on him who conspired against his lord.

DAY 13: F. F. F. Satisfying the heart of the great gods with a feast, and saluting their lord who overthrew the enemies, and they will exist no more.

DAY 14: F. F. F. It is the day of receiving the white crown by the Majesty of Horus; his Ennead is in great festivity. Offer to your local gods, and pacify the spirits.

DAY 15: F. A. A. Do not go out of your house at eventide. Going forth of (the Majesty of) Ra at (nightfall with his followers).If any person sees them he will pass away (immediately).

(DAY 16: (......)   Feast of (Osiris-Onnophris..), the gods who are in his retinue are in great festivity; the Ennead, their (hearts) being pleased. If you see anything on this day, it will be good.

DAY 17: F. F. F. Smelling ...on this day by the great Ennead and the little Ennead who come forth from Nun. Give up bread and beer. Burn incense to Ra and an invocation-offering to the spirits. It is important so that your words may be listened to by your local gods.

DAY 18: A. A. A. Do not do any (thing) on this day. It is the day Anubis inspected the wabet (w‘bt), while Seth was (making) transformations into lizards in the sight of (all men)... he found. . . being examined to care for burial. Then he started weeping; then he repeated it (i.e. weeping) as he had seen. Thereupon, they started weeping aloud. They placed their hands on their heads; the gods, males and females, likewise.

DAY 19: F. F. F. It is the day of the going forth of Nun to set up the noble one in his place in order to give compensation to the gods who are in the presence of the noble one.

DAY 20: A. A. A. It is the day of giving the compensation in the presence of Ra, and the conducting by Thoth accordingly it is making an example thereof in overthrowing the rebels against their lord. Then they carried off Seth, son of Nut; and they shall be underneath—so said the gods.

Abramelin:

Mahra, Rascheä, Nogah, Adae, Erimites,

Trapi, Naga, Echami, Aspadit, Nasi,

5. Peḥui-tchat.

5. PEḤUI-TCHAT

(6th Decan)
Akhet month II
Season of Inundation
3rd Trimester (circa. September)

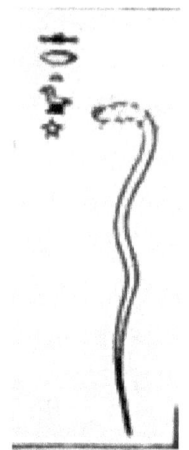

Egyptian name:

Phewy djat (*pḥwy ḏ3t*)

"Tail balancer"

Image:

Erect serpent

Mineral:

Galena and Gold

Aspect:

DAY 21: A. A. F. It is the day of the going forth of the Upper Egyptian Neith in the presence of the Majesty of (Atum Ra-Hor)akhti—may he live and be prosperous. It is her eyes which guided Thoth in appeasing and praising the Upper Egyptian goddess.

DAY 22: A. A. A. Do not bathe on this day. It is the day of cutting the tongue of the enemy of Sobek, thy son (i.e. son of Neith).

DAY 23: F. A. A. Anyone born on this day will die of a crocodile.

DAY 24: A. A. A. Do not go out of your house on it in any wind until Ra sets. (It is the day) of the going forth of the executioners from Sais of the Delta to look for the children of Bedesh (Apophis) when he is in the ocean. If any lion glances at it (or : them), he will pass away immediately.

DAY 25: A. A. A. (Do not) go out on it (i.e. this day) on any road. It is the day of finding the children of (Apophis) wrapped in [the archaic way] on a mat on (their) sides ... in his charge... (If any lion) looks for the gods on this day, he will suffer from the trampling of a bull on it (i.e. this day) until he dies.

DAY 26: A. A. A. Do not put the foundation of a house. [See Dreambook III viii 24] Do not put (a ship) in a shipyard. Do not order any work. Do not do any work on this day. It is the day of opening and sealing the windows of the palace of Busiris.

DAY 27: A. A. A. Do not go out. Do not give your back to any work until the sun sets. As to anyone born on this day he will die by a snake,

DAY 28: F. F. F. If you see anything [in the night sky], it will be good on this day.

DAY 29: F. F. F. Anyone born on this day will die as an honourable man among (his people).

LAST DAY: (F. F. F.) . . . . . Found missing.(.....) by Nun, father of the gods; the land is in festivity on (this day).

Abramelin:

Peralit, Emfalion, Paruch, Girmil, Tolet,

Helmis, Asinel, Ionion, Asturel, Flabiscon,

6. Themat-ḥert.

6. THEMAT-HERT

(7th Decan)
Akhet Month III
Season of Inundation
1st Trimester
(Circa. September)

Egyptian name:

Temat heret kheret (*tm3t hrt hrt*)
"State of peace"

Image:

Lion-headed Goddess,
Uraeus or disk on head,
seated, scepter & ankh.

Mineral:

Glass and Gold

Aspect:

DAY 1: F. F. F. Feast of the mistress of heaven, Hathor in heaven ....gods . . . mistress of all female gods.

DAY 2: (BLANK). Return of Wedjoyet from Dep in order to transmit ....

DAY 3: F. F. F. (. . .) by the noble god. If you see anything, it will be good on this day.

DAY 4 : A. A. A. Trembling of the earth under Nun. If anyone navigates on this day, his house (will be destroyed).

DAY 5: A. A. A. Do not keep fire burning in the house on this day. Do not look at it on this day. It is the day of blaming ... by the Majesty of this god.

DAY 6: F. F. F. The encouragement of the gods of the two lands [Horus & Seth] on this day . . .encouragement of ... the whole land (on this day).

DAY 7: F. F. F. If you see anything, (it will be good) on this day.

DAY 8: (NO SPACE) Isis goes forth — her heart being pleased on this day, the heritage being established unto her son, Horus.

DAY 9: A. A. A. Do not go outside on any road from your house on this day. Do not let light fall on your face until Ra sets in his horizon. It is the day of blaming the great ones. FOUND MISSING who were in his presence.

DAY 10: F. F. F. Great rejoicing in heaven; the crew of Ra are in peace, his Ennead is cheerful. Those in the fields are working.

Abramelin:

Nascela, Conioli, Isnirki, Pliroki, Aslotama,

Zagriona, Parmasa, Sarasi, Geriola, Afonono,

7. Themat-khert.

7. THEMAT-KHERT . .

(8th Decan)
Akhet month III
season of inundation
2nd Trimester (circa. sep - oct)

Egyptian name:

Weshatei bekati (*wš3t(i) bk3t(i)*)

"Pregnant widgeon"

Image:

a serpent with human arms and legs, standing, offering two nw-jars.

Mineral: Turquoise

Aspect:

DAY 11: F. F. F. If you see anything, it will be good.

DAY 12: (NO SPACE) The pacification of the heart of the gods wherever they are, the wedjat—eye being on the head of Ra. Fixing . . . (for the gods). Raising those who are upon their seats.

DAY 13 : A. A. A. It is the day of cutting into pieces ... ferrymen (?) on the river for not ferrying over the confederates of Seth. . .any. . .against this neshmet-boat of Osiris which is sailing upstream to Abydos to the great town of Onnophris. Behold, he (sic) is transformed into a little old person in the arms of (his ?) nurse. . .giving gold as a reward to Nemty[16] as a fare saying : Pray, ferry (me) over to the west; then he received it from him...because of announcing the divine limbs. Behold, the confederates were following him like a swarm of reptiles. Thereupon, they (recognised) these gods, while Seth entered into the embalming booth. . .to announce the god's limbs. Then they became fresh. . . he came. . . as enemy on water following him, having transformed themselves into small cattle. Then these gods made a terrible massacre. They divided them among the crew. Then offering was made from the tongue of the enemy of

Nemty in order to approach the gold in the house of Nemty to this day. One wondered at the small cattle on the west. One wondered at transforming the small cattle into flocks until this day.

DAY 14: A. A. A. Do not do anything on this day. The heart of the gods is sad because of that which has been done by the enemy of Nemty. Anyone born on this day will die of...

DAY 15: A. A. A. Inspecting by Ba-neb-djedet (the lusty bull)... in the sacred temple.

DAY 16: F. F. F. The appearance of the great ones in Ashmunein. Bringing of Ibis ... establishing ... in Ashmunein. A happy day of infinity and eternity.

DAY 17: A. A. A. (Landing) of the great ones, the upper and lower ones at Abydos; loud weeping and wailing by Isis and Nephthys, her sister, over Onnophris in Sais. It (i.e. weeping and crying) (is heard) in Abydos.

DAY 18: A. A. A. It is the day of the strife by the children of Geb. Seth and sister... Do not approach any road for making a journey on this day.

DAY 19: A. A. A. The children of the storm (Apophis or Seth) of ... Do not sail downstream or upstream on the river. Do not navigate any boat on this day.

DAY 20: A. A. A. The going forth of Bastet, mistress of Ankh-towe in front of Ra, she being angry. The god could not stand in her neighbourhood. Anyone born on this day will die in the year of pestilence.

8. Usthá.

Abramelin:

Liriell, Alagill, Opollogon, Carubot, Morilon, Losimon, Kagaros, Ygilon, Gesegos, Ugefor.

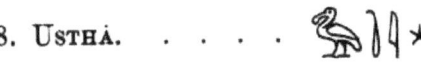

(9th decan)
Akhet month III
Season of inundation
3rd Trimester (circa. October)

Egyptian name:

Ipesed or ipedejs (*Ipsd, ipds*)

"Tail balancer, reckoner"

Image:

Erect serpent

Mineral:

Iron and gold

Aspect:

DAY 21: F. F. F. The feast of Shu, son of Ra. It is the day of Rennutet in the mesektet-boat.

DAY 22: (NO SPACE) Raising Maat in order to see Ra when she is summoned by the gods in the presence of Ra. A uraeus was placed upon her, and another below her, being fixed at the front of the mesektet-boat.

DAY 23: A. A. A. Nun drags .... by their hands out of the fire. Behold, the Majesty of this god judges in that great place ... on the river. Anyone born on this day will not live.

DAY 24: F. F. F. Isis goes forth, her heart being happy and Nephthys being also in jubilation when they see Onnophris ... heart. He has given his throne to his son, Horus in front of Ra.

DAY 25: F. F. F. If you see anything, it will be good on the heart of the gods.

DAY 26: F. F. F. Establishing the Djed of Atum in the heaven and land, of Heliopolis (at the moment) of uproar. Reconciliation of the two lords and causing the land to be in peace. The whole of Egypt is given to Horus, and all the desert land to Seth. Going forth of Thoth in order to judge in the presence of Ra.

DAY 27: F.F.F. Judging Horus and Seth; stopping the fighting. Hunting down the rowers and putting an end to the uproar. Satisfying the two lords and causing the two doors to open.

DAY 28: F. F. F. The gods are in jubilation and in joy when the will is written for Horus, son of Osiris to propitiate Onnophris in the necropolis. Then the land is in festivity and the gods are pleased. If you see anything, it will be good.

DAY 29: F. F. F. The going forth of the three noble ladies who are in the Tanenet sanctuary in the presence of Ptah, beautiful of face, while giving praise to Ra, him who belongs to the throne of truth of the temples of the goddesses. Giving the white crown to Horus, and the red one to Seth.[usually said to be otherway round] Their hearts are pleased there with.

LAST DAY: F. F. F. If you see anything, it will be good on this day.

Abramelin:

Asoreg, Paruchu, Siges, Atherom, Ramara,

Jajaregi, Golema, Kiliki, Romasara, Alpaso,

9. Bekatha.

9. BEKATHÁ . . . .

(10th decan)
Akhet month IV
Season of inundation
1st trimester (circa. October)

Egyptian name:
Sebeshsen or sebehes (*sbšsn, sbḥs*)
"Double Vessel Star"

Image:
Lion-headed Goddess, Uraeus or disk on head, seated with two flagella

Mineral: Glass and Gold

Aspect
House of Ra (tomorrow)
House of Osiris (yesterday)
House of Horus (today)

DAY 1: F. F. F. The great Ennead and the (small) Ennead went to propitiate the Majesty of Nun in the cavern. The Majesty of Thoth ordered Sia and (his followers)...saying: A copy of the order of the Majesty of Ra saying to his father Nun: This command of the Majesty of Ra Atum is brought to thee. Ra is joyful in his beauty, his Ennead is in festivity. Everybody, every lion and every single one (lit. every nose of his) among the protective (ʿnḥy) serpent: gods, goddesses, spirits (akhw), dead and those who came into being in the primordial age, thy form is in every body of thine.

DAY 2: F. F. F. (above line). Gods and goddesses are in festivity; the heaven and the land are in joy. If you see anything [in the sky], (it will be) good on this day.

DAY 3: A. A. A. Do not do anything on this day. It is the day of smashing *(skri)* into the ears of Bata within his own inaccessible temples. Anyone born on this day will die of (his) ears.

DAY 4: F. F. F. One should perform the rituals in the temple of Sokar and in thy house (on) this day, with all provisions in the necropolis — they will be pleasant to the gods on this day.

DAY 5: F. F. F. The going forth of Hathor (Khentet-abet) in the presence of the great ones in the battlefield (Kher-'aha). Life, stability and welfare are given to her and the Ennead and the gods of battlefield; and the Majesty of Inundation, father of the gods, is in great festivity on this day.

DAY 6: A. A. A. (Do not go out on this day)... when the barque of Ra (is established) in order to (overthrow Apophis from one moment to another on this) day.

DAY 7: A. A. A. It is the day of... wind...death in... He will turn into...fish. Do not eat or taste (?) mehyet-fish.. on this day.

DAY 8: F. F. F. If you see anything [in the sky], it will be good on this day.

DAY 9: F. F. F. It is the day of the action performed by Thoth. Speech by the Majesty of Ra in the presence of the great ones. Thereupon, these gods together with Thoth caused (Apophis) the enemy of Seth to kill himself in his sanctuary. It is this that has been done by the executioners of Qesert (Apophis) until this day.

DAY 10: F. F. F. As to anyone born on this day (he will die in old age while beer enters into his mouth), his eyes and his face.

Abramelin:

Soteri, Amillee, Ramage, Pormatho, Metosee, Porascho, Anamil, Orienell, Timiran, Oramos,

10. Ṭepā-Khentet.

10. Ṭepā-khentet . .

(11th decan)
Akhet month IV
Season of inundation
2nd trimester
(circa. Oct - Nov)

Egyptian name:

Tepy-'khenet (*tpy-ꜥhnt*)

"Cup star (head of)"

Image:

human headed Goddess with outstretched arms, as though seated but with no support

Mineral:

Haematite

Aspect:

DAY 11: F. F. F. Feast of Osiris in Abydos in the great neshmet-boat on this day. The dead are in jubilation.

DAY 12: A. A. A. Do not go out on it (i.e. this day) on any road in the wind. It is the day of the transformation into *Benu*. Offer to the *Benu* in your house on this day

day 13: F. F. F. The going forth of the white one (Hathor) of heaven, their heart being pleased in the presence of Ra. The great Ennead is in festivity. Make a holiday in your house on this day.

DAY 14: F. F. F. The goddesses of weaving (Hedj-hotpe and the Tayet) come forth from the temple of Benben on this day. They handed over things to (Neith) on this day. Their hearts are happy.

DAY 15: . . . (Do not). . . of. . . another. *Ndmyt* in order to bring. . . .

DAY 16: . . .Feast of Sekhmet (and Bastet) in. . . Ra. Behold.

Day 17: A. A. F. The people and the gods judge the speech of the crew(?) in Heliopolis when Horus arrives on the battlefield (*Kher-ˁ3hˁ*). Do not go out at midday on this day.

Day 18 : A. A. A. is the day of overthrowing the boat of the god on this day.

Day 19 : A. A. A. Presenting of offering in the Red Room *(Hwt-dsrt)*. Making ointment for Osiris before the hall of embalmment. Do not taste bread and beer on this day. Drink water (i.e. juice) of the grapes until Ra sets.

Day 20 : A. A. A. Do not go out on any road on this day. Do not anoint thyself with ointment on this day. It is the day of looking in the direction of the Akhet-eye (sun). Do not go out of your house at midday.

Abramelin:

Anemalon, Kirek, Batamabub, Ranar, Namalon,
Ampholion, Abusis, Egention, Tabori, Concario,

11. Khentet-ḥert.

11. Khentet-hert . .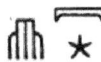

(12th decan)
Akhet Month IV
Season of Inundation
3rd Trimester (circa. November)

Egyptian name:

Khenetet horet (ẖnt(t) ḥr(t))

"To the tomb by sky or water"

Image:

Erect serpent

Mineral:

Dark Quartz and Gold

Aspect:

DAY 21 : A. A. F. It is the day of the going forth of the mysterious great ones to look for the Akhet-eye (sun). Do not go out of your house in day-time.

DAY 22 : F. F. F. If you see anything it will be good on this day. .

DAY 23 : F. F. A. Do not go out during night-time. . . in heaven. . . They. . . in order to annihilate. . . Horus, the saviour of his father.

DAY 24: If you see (any lion), you will pass away at his hands (or, immediately).

DAY 25 : missing

DAY 26: . . .F. Thoth establishes the nobles in an advanced position in Letopolis.

DAY 27: F. F. A. If you see anything, it will be good. Do not go out at night-time on this day.

DAY 28: A. A. A. Do not eat any mehyet-fish on this day. Do not offer on it (namely, on this day). It is the day of the going forth of the hat-mehyet-fish which is in Busiris, its form being an iten-fish (i.e. a dolphin).

DAY 29: A. A. A. Do not eat or smell any mehyet-fish while throwing flame into water from what they offer (and which they take upon their hands) of any mehyet-fish (or, any kind of fish).

LAST DAY: F. F. F. If you see anything, it will be pleasing to the heart of the gods and goddesses on this day. Offer to the gods and the assistants of the Ennead. Make an invocation offering to the spirits, and give food in accordance with their list. It is the day of the pleasure of the great Ennead.

Abramelin:

Golemi, Tarato, Tabbata, Buriuh, Omana,

Caraschi, Dimurga, Kogid, Panfodra, Siria,

12. Khentet-khert.

12. **KHENTET-KHERT** .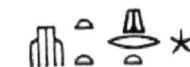

(13th Decan)
Peret month 1
Winter season
1st trimester (circa. Nov)

Egyptian name:

Khenetet kheret (ẖnt(t) ẖrt)

Image:

Lion-headed Goddess, Uraeus on head, seated with sistrum and flagellum. Or lion-headed God, standing, hands on heads of two monkeys squatted on supports.

Mineral:

Red jasper and gold

Aspect:

House of Ra (tomorrow)

House of Osiris (yesterday)

House of Horus (today)

DAY 1 : F. F. F. Double the offerings and present the gifts of Nehebkau to the gods in the presence of Ptah in the shrines of Ta-nenet of goddesses and gods, saviours of Ra and his own followers, and the. . . of Ptah-Sokar and Sekhmet the great, Nefertem, Horus-Hekenu, Mahes, Bastet, the great fire …. propitiating the Wedjat-eye. It will be good.

DAY 2: F. . . . offering before. . . in. . . nourishment. . . (Make a holiday in your house).

DAY 3: …. Do not burn fire in the presence of Ra , . . . everybody.

DAY 4 : F. F. F. If you see anything, it will be good. Anyone born on this day will die old among his people. He will spend a (long) life-time, and he would be received by his father.

DAY 5 : F. A. A. It is the day of placing the flame in front of the great ones by Sekhmet who presides in the Lower Egyptian sanctuary when she was violent in her manifestations because of her detention in it (i.e. the sanctuary) by Maat, Ptah, Thoth, Hu and Sia, the gods on this day. . . of everyday on this day.

DAY 6 : F. F. F. Repeat the offerings of the victuals of him who dwells in the holy place (*Weret*), and return the victuals of the noble Khenti-irty, and offerings to the gods were doubled by everyone on this day.

DAY 7: A. A. A. Do not have intercourse with any woman or any person in front of the great flame (i.e. the sun) which is in your house on this day.

DAY 8: F. F. F. If you see anything, it will be good on this day.

DAY 9: F. F. F. The gods are joyful with the offerings of Sekhmet [on this] day. Establish the *cakes of light (p3wt)*[17] and repeat the offerings. It will be pleasant; to the heart of the gods and the spirits.

DAY 10: A. A. A. (Do not) burn any papyrus on this day. It is the day of the coming forth of flame (together with Horus from the marshes) on this day.

Abramelin:

Igigi, Dosom, Darachin,
Horomor, Ahahbon,
Yraganon, Lagiros, Eralier,
Golog, Cemiel,

☆ ☆ ☆

13. Themes-en-khentet.

13. THEMES-EN-KHENTET

(14th Decan)
Peret month 1
Winter season
2nd trimester
(circa. Nov - Dec)

Egyptian name:

Tems khenetet (*tms ḫnt(t)*)

"Man God, strong armed who grasps you"

Image:

Lion headed God standing

Mineral:

Glass and Gold

Aspect:

DAY 11: A. A. A. Do not (approach) flame on this day. . . and. . . on this day. . .

DAY 12: A. A. A. If you see any dog (on this day), do not approach him on the day of answering every speech of Sekhmet on this day.

DAY 13: F. F. F. Prolonging life-time and making beneficent the goddess of truth in the temple.

DAY 14: A. A. A. Lamentations of Isis and Nephthys. It is the day when they mourned Osiris in Busiris in remembrance of that which he had seen. Do not listen to singing and chanting on this day.

DAY 15: F. F. F. If you see anything [in the sky], it will be good on this day. It is the day of the going forth of Nun through the cave to the place (where the gods are). . . (in) darkness.

DAY 16 : F. F. F. Going forth of Shu in order to count the crew of the mesektet-boat.

DAY 17: A. A. A. Do not wash yourself with water on this day. It is the day of the going forth of Nun to the place where the gods are. Those who are above and below come into existence; the land being (still) in chaos.

DAY 18: F. F. F. A day (i.e. holiday) in Rostau. The going forth of the gods to Abydos.

DAY 19: A. A. A. The great gods are in heaven on this day and (lit. mixed with) the pestilence of the year. Many deaths are in it (i.e. this day). If it passes by anyone, he will not recover from the disease which is in him.

DAY 20: A. A. A. Do not do anything on this day. It is the day of the going forth of Bastet who protects the two lands and cares for him who comes in darkness. Beware of passing on land until Ra sets.

Abramelin:

Hagus, Vollman, Bialode, Galago, Bagoloni,
Tmako, Akanejohano, Argaro, Afrei, Sagara,

14. Sapt-khennu.

14. SAPT-KHENNU

(15th Decan)
Peret month 1
Winter Season
3rd Trimester (circa. December)

Egyptian name:

Septy henewy, *(spt(y) ḥnwy)* "singer"

Image:

Erect serpent

Mineral:

Flint

Aspect:

DAY 20: A. A. A. Do not do anything on this day. It is the day of the going forth of Bastet who protects the two lands and cares for him who comes in darkness. Beware of passing on land until Ra sets.

DAY 21: F. F. F. Guidance of the two lands by Bastet, and making a Abt-offering to the followers (*i.e.* of Ra) on this day.

DAY 22: F. F. F. If you see anything [in the sky], it will be good on this day.

DAY 23: F. F. F. Anyone born on this day will die in great old age and rich in every good thing.

DAY 24: F. F. F. Everything has been placed behind him in the presence of the (Ennead) (on) the occasion of being loyal to the executioners of Ra. Happiness is in heaven and on earth on this day.

DAY 25: (NO SPACE) Do not eat milk on this day. Establishing of the great divine cow in the presence of the Majesty of Ra. Drink and eat honey on this day.

DAY 26: A. A. A. Do not go out on it (*i.e.* this day) until Ra sets when offerings are diminished in Busiris, while they are put on earth towards heaven. They will be much blamed about it.

DAY 27: F. F. F. Great festivity in Hefau. . .??. . . .in festivity. . . on this day.

DAY 28: F. F. F. (of Horus & Seth not to fight) taking a solemn oath by Thoth in Ashmunein, and the going forth of the noble one. The land is in festivity on this day. Make a holiday in your house.

DAY 29: F. F. F. Appearance in the sight of Hu. Thoth will send this command southwards to guide the two lands by Bastet together with the sole mistress, Sekhmet the great, the gods being happy. If you see anything, it will be good on this day.

LAST DAY: F. F. F. Crossing over in the presence of Nun from the temple of Hapi, the father of the gods and the Ennead, Lords of the Battlefield (Kher-'aha). Do not neglect them while incense is on the fire according to their list *on* this day.

Abramelin:

Ugali, Erimihala, Hatuny, Hagomi, Opilon,

Paguldez, Paschy, Nimalon, Horog, Algebol,

15. Ḥer-åb-uåa.

15. Ḥer-ab-uåa . . .

(16th Decan)
Peret month 2
Winter season
1st trimester (circa. December)

Egyptian name:

Hery-ib wia (*ḥry-ib wiȝ*)

"who dwells in the middle of the sacred bark"

Image:

Lion-headed Goddess,

Mineral:

Lapis Lazuli and Gold

Aspect:

House of Ra (tomorrow)

House of Osiris (yesterday)

House of Horus (today)

DAY 1: F. F. F. The gods and goddesses are in festivity on this day, (namely), in the feast of (lifting) the heaven of Ra by Ptah with his hands (he who has no equal). A holiday in the entire land.

DAY 2: F.F.F. The day of receiving Ra by the gods. The heart of the two lands is in festivity.

DAY 3: A. A. A. Do not go out of your house on any road on this day. (It is the day of) the going forth of Seth together with his confederates to the eastern horizon, and the navigation of Maat to the place (where the gods are).

DAY 4: F. F. F. Apply your heart to your local gods; propitiate your spirits (akhw); exalt your crew during the day on this day.

DAY 5: F. F. F. If you see anything [in the sky], it will be good on this day.

DAY 6: A. A. A. It is the day of putting up the Djed by the Majesty of Osiris. Then the gods were sad with (their) faces downwards when they remember the Majesty of this god. They pronounced those who were before.

DAY 7: F. F. F. Make invocation offering to the spirits (akhw) in your house. Make the great (*3ᶜbt*) offering to the gods, and they will be accepted on this day.

DAY 8: F. F. F. Make a holiday in Letopolis. The gods and goddesses are in festivity on this day.

DAY 9: F. F. F. The god enters as he will conduct this rationing and all the gods of the battlefield (*Kher-ᶜ3h3*). If you see anything [in the sky], it will be good on this day.

DAY 10: A. A. A. The going forth of the Wedjat-eye for singing in Heliopolis. Raising up of the (female) Majesty of the sanctuary by Mnevis. Ra raised Maat again and again to Atum.

Abramelin:

Rigolon, Trasorim, Elason, Trisacha, Gagolchon,

Klorecha, Irachro, Pafessa, Amami, Camalo.

16. Shesmu.

16. SHESMU

(17th Decan)
Peret month 2
Winter season
2nd trimester (circa. Dec - Jan)

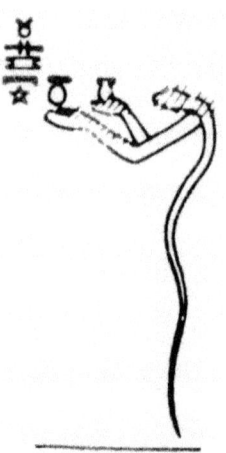

Egyptian name:

Seshemew (*sšmw*)

"Guiding serpent of God."

Image: :

Serpent with human arms and legs, standing, offering two nw-jars.

Mineral:

Glass and Gold

Aspect:

DAY 11: F. F. F. Feast of Neith in Sais, and taking the writing material that was prepared in her house. The going forth of Sobek to guide her Majesty. Thou wilt see good (at) her hands.

DAY 12: F. F. F. If you see anything, it will be good on this day.

DAY 13: A. A. A. Do not go out of your house on any road on this day. It is the day of the proceeding of Sekhmet to Letopolis (?) Her great executioners passed by the offering of Letopolis on this day.[15]

DAY 14: A. F. F. Do not go out on it (i.e. this day) at the beginning of dawn. It is the day of seeing the rebel (Apophis) and killing him by Seth at the prow of the great barque.

DAY 15: (APPARENTLY BLANK) The gods go forth for him in heaven. His two hands holding the *ankh* and *was* which he gives to *Khenty-irty* at the time of his reckoning.

DAY 16: (B L A N K) ...Awakening of Isis by the Majesty of Ra... their hands when the son Horus saved his father. He has beaten Seth and his confederates.

DAY 17: F. F. F. It is the day of keeping those things of the *wabet* of Osiris which have been placed in the hands of Anubis.

DAY 18: A. A. A. The going forth of the seven executioners in *R-hesert*, their fingers are searching for the Akhet-eye in the town of Iyet and Letopolis.

DAY 19: F. A. A. Do not decide yourself to go during daytime. It is the day of (mourning the god), (blank)

DAY 20: A. A. A. The proceeding of the (female) Majesty of heaven southward to the road...

Abramelin:

Taxae, Karase, Riqita, Schulego, Giria,

Afimo, Bafa, Baroa, Golog, Iromoni,

17. Kenmu.

17. KENMU

(18th Decan)
PERET MONTH 2
WINTER SEASON
3RD TRIMESTER (CIRCA. JANUARY)

Egyptian name:
Kenemew (*knm(w)*) "Coiled One"

Image:
Uraeus serpent coiled on a support

Mineral:
Gold and Carnelian

Aspect:

DAY 21 : (BLANK) Birth of the cattle... to the place where the meadows are in the neighbourhood of this foremost god.

DAY 22: F. F. F. If you see anything [in the sky], it will be good on this day.

DAY 23: F. F. F. If you see anything [in the sky], it will be good on this day.

DAY 24: A. A. A. Do not sail in a boat on this day. The gods are descending into the river. As to anyone who approaches on it (i.e. this day) on the river, he will not live.

DAY 25: F. F. F. If you see anything [in the sky], it will be good (on this day).

DAY 26 : (BLANK) Going forth of Min from Coptos on this day. He is guided to it; boasting about his beauty (phallus?). Isis saw that his face was beautiful.

DAY 27: (NO SPACE) Feast of Sokar in Rostau before (that of) Onnophris in Abydos.

DAY 28: F. F. F. Onnophris is pleased and the spirits are joyful, the dead are also in festivity.

DAY 29: A. A. A. Instigation of fighting, creation of rebellion and making uproar among the children of Geb. Do not do anything on this day.

LAST DAY: A. A. A. Do not raise your voice on this day.

Abramelin:

Pigios, Nimtrix, Herich, Akirgi, Tapum,

Hipolopos, Hosun, Garses, Ugirpon, Gomognu.

18. Semṭet.

(19th Decan)
peret month 3
winter season
1st trimester (circa. january)

Egyptian name:

Tepy semd (*tpyꜥ semd*) "Left Ear" perhaps one who whispers in one's ear.

Image:

Lion-headed Goddess, Uraeus on head, seated, scepter and ankh.

Mineral :

Gold

Aspect:

House of Ra (tomorrow)

House of Osiris (yesterday)

House of Horus (today)

Day 1: F. F. F. It is the day of ... in heaven and on earth and everybody likewise. Feast of entering into heaven and the two banks. Horus is jubilating.

Day 2: F. F. F. If you see anything [in the sky], it will be (good on) this day.

Day 3: ... (blank) ...

Day 4: F. A. A. Announcement of fighting; call in Heliopolis by Seth; his voice being in heaven, his voice being on earth, through great fury.

Day 5: F. F. F. Neith goes forth from Sais when they see (her) beauty in the night for four and half (hours). Do not go out in them (i.e. these hours).

DAY 6: F. F. F. Jubilation of Osiris in Busiris; going forth of Anubis, (his) adorers (or, adoration) following him; he has received everybody in the hall. Mayest thou make the ritual

DAY 7: A. A. A. Do not go out of your house until Ra sets. It is the day when *the* eye of Ra called the followers, and they reached him (in) the evening. Beware of it!

DAY 8: F. F. F. If you see anything [in the sky], it will be good on this day. It is the day *of* making way for the gods by Khnum who presides over those who remove themselves from him.

DAY 9: F. F. F. Judgement in Heliopolis.

DAY 10: A. A. A. It is the day of the coming of Thoth. They guided the very great Flame (Nesert) into her house of the desert of eternity (along) the way which she has found among them. As to anyone who approaches her on this day, thou (sic) shalt not be separated from her by violence.

Abramelin:

Argilo, Tardoe, Cepacha, Kalote, Ychniag,

Basanola, Nachero, Natolisa, Mesah, Mesadu,

19. Ṭepā-semṭ.

19. Ṭepā-semṭ

(20TH DECAN)
PERET MONTH 3
WINTER SEASON
2ND TRIMESTER
(CIRCA. JAN - FEB)

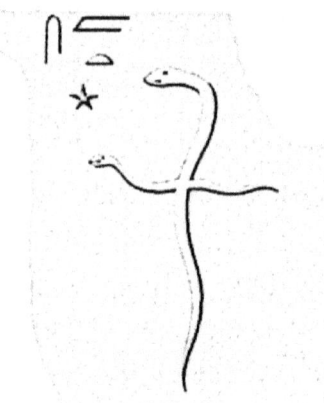

Egyptian name:

Semed (*smd*) "accusation or complaint"

Image:

Erect serpent with another serpent crossing its body

Mineral:

Copper and Gold

Aspect:

DAY 11: F. F. F. As to the dead who go about in the necropolis on this day, the dead are (going about) in order to repel the anger of the enemy who is in the said land.

DAY 12: F. F. F. The Nile (*wsr-hat*) comes from Nun on this day. Victuals are being given on this day.

DAY 13: F. F. F. Coming of Thoth (with his spirits) on this day. Replacing ... in the seats of the goddesses. As to any ritual action, it will be good on this day.

DAY 14: A. A. (SIC) Do not go out of your house (on any road) on this day. It is the day of making health (the life time in Letopolis).

DAY 15: A. A. A. Rebellion in the shrine (?) Do not do any work on this day.

DAY 16: A. A. A. Opening of the windows and opening of the court, and looking into the doorways of Karnak, where his place is. Do not see darkness on this day.

DAY 17: A. A. A. Do not pronounce the name of Seth on this day. As to him who pronounces his name without his knowledge, he will not stop from fighting in his house eternally.

DAY 18: F. F. F. Feast of Nut who counts the days. Make a holiday (in) your house.

DAY 19: (NO SPACE) Birth of Nut anew ... (good) any dead on (this) day. . . Bastet... the Majesty of the foreign land. Do not go out of your house; do not see light.

DAY 20: A. A. A. Do not go out of your house on any road. Do not see light *(sw)*.

Abramelin:
Capipa, Fermetu, Barnel, Ubarim, Urgivoh,
Ysquiron, Odac, Rotor, Arator, Butharusch.

20. Sert.

20. SERT . . . . .

(21st decan)
Peret month III
WINTER SEASON
3RD TRIMESTER
(CIRCA. FEBRUARY)

Egyptian name:

Sert (*srt*), "Backbone"

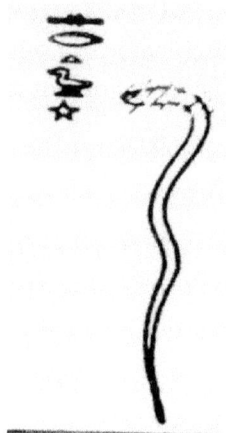

Image :

Erect serpent

Mineral:

Dark Flint and Gold

Aspect:

(DAY 21: dropped).

DAY 22: A. A. A. Birth of the mysterious one (Apophis) with his limbs. Do not get the thought of pronouncing the name of the snakes. It is the day of catching his children in Dep.

DAY 23: F. F. F. Feast of Horus in *kem-wer* on this day of his years in his very beautiful images.

DAY 24: A. A. A. Do not go out of your house on any road on this day.

DAY 25: (NO SPACE) Do not do anything on this day because -of the great cry which the gods of Djesert-(places) made, having come this day.

DAY 26: A. A. A. He was sent into the cave without the knowledge of the great ones (?). . . to look for the occasion of coming on this day.

DAY 27: A. A. A. Do not do anything on this day.

DAY 28: F. F. F. (Feast of) Osiris in Abydos. The Majesty of Onnophris puts up the *twryt-tree*.

DAY 29: F. F. F. If you see anything, it will be good.

LAST DAY:... Feast in Busiris. The names of the doorways (of the horizon) come into existence.

Abramelin:

Harkinson, Arabim, Koreh, Forsterton, Sernpolo, Magelucha, Amagestol, Sikesti, Mechebbera, Tigrapho.

21. Sasa-Sert.

(22nd Decan)
Peret month 4
Winter season
1st trimester (circa. February)

Egyptian name:

Sa sert (*s3 srt*) "Behind one's back"

Image:

Lion-headed Goddess, Uraeus on head, seated, scepter and ankh

Mineral:

Carnelian and Gold

Aspect:

House of Ra (tomorrow)

House of Osiris (yesterday)

House of Horus (today)

DAY 1: F. F. F. Great feast (in heaven). It is the day of smiting the enemy as rebels against their mistress on this day.

DAY 2: F. F. F. The Majesty of Geb proceeds to the throne of Busiris to see Anubis, who commands the council on the requirements (of the day).

DAY 3: A. A. A. Do not do anything on this day. Fighting of the great ones with the Uraeus, appointing her on the spot to make grow (lit. create) this eye of Horus the Elder. As for any lion who pronounces the name of the Decan-Orion he will pass away at once.

DAY 4: F. F. F. If you see anything, it will be good on this day. The gods and goddesses are satisfied when they see the children of Geb sitting in their places.

DAY 5: A. A. A. The Majesty of Horus is well when the Red Goddess sees his form. As for anybody who approaches on it (i.e. this day), anger will start on it (i.e. this day).

DAY 6: A. A. A. Going forth of the stars, (culminating) bitterly and openly. If anybody sees the small cattle, he will pass away at once.

DAY 7: F. F. F. (The going forth) of Min into the tent, l. p. h. (life, prosperity and health) in festivity. The gods are jubilating. Pay attention to the incense on the fire. Smell (or, smelling of) sweet myrrh.

DAY 8: F. F. F. The Ennead is in adoration when (they see) this eye of (Horus) the Elder in its place. Revised are all its parts (½, ¼ etc) in it in counting it for its master.

DAY 9: A. A. A. Do not go out on it (at the time of) darkness when (Ra) goes in it. . . its name. . . (lacuna). It is the day of. . . (introducing) the great ones before Ra (to the wholeness of the *wedjet*) . . . (If) you see (anything, it will be good on this day).

DAY 10: (Do not) go out of your house (on any road) on this day.

Abramelin:

Malata, Tagora, Petuna,
Amia, Somi,
Lotogi, Hyris, Chadail,
Debam, Abagrion.

22. Kher-khept-sert.

(23RD DECAN)
PERET MONTH 4
WINTER SEASON
2ND TRIMESTER (CIRCA. FEB - MAR)

Egyptian name:

Hery heped sert (*ḥry ḥpd srt*)

"Master of those coming from below"

Image:

Erect winged serpent

Mineral:

Glass and Gold, sometimes Silver

Aspect:

DAY 11: A. A. A. .. (gods) of the shrines in the temple ....

DAY 12: A. A. A. As to him who sees dancing, or digging on any road... do not approach (?) the Majesty of Montu... in digging (or dancing) and do not look at it at all ...

DAY 13: A. A. A. . . .any wind on this day. It is the day of conducting Osiris. . . his ship to Abydos (on this day).

DAY 14: A. A. A. The crew go about the gods on this day to look for (the confederates of Seth). Do not be courageous (on this day).

DAY 15: F. F. F. A great happy day in the eastern horizon of heaven when instructions were given to the followers of the gods in their temples in the presence of the great ones in the two horizons.

DAY 16: F. F. F. Going forth of Khepra who hears the words of his followers there. Every town is in joy.

DAY 17: A. A. A. Going forth of Seth, son of Nut, to disturb the great ones who check him in his town of *Sw* (in Heracleopolitan nome). Now these gods recognized him, and they repelled his followers, none of them remained.

DAY 18: A. A. A. Do not approach (when the Majesty of) Ra goes forth. Do not wash yourself with water on this day.

DAY 19: F. F. F. The Majesty of (Ra) goes forth (in his barque. . .) heaven. Feast. . . in Heliopolis. (If you see anything, it will be) good on this day.

DAY 20: A. A. A. Do not (do any work on) this day while he (repels those who rebel) against their master. As to anyone who passes (them, he will suffer from the trampling of a bull *herey-ka*) to infinity.

Abramelin:

Paschan, Cobel, Arioth, Panari, Caboneton,

Kamual, Erytar, Nearah, Hahadu, Charagi.

23. Khukhu.

23. KHUKHU . . . .

(24th Decan)
Peret month 4
Winter season
3rd trimester
(circa. March)

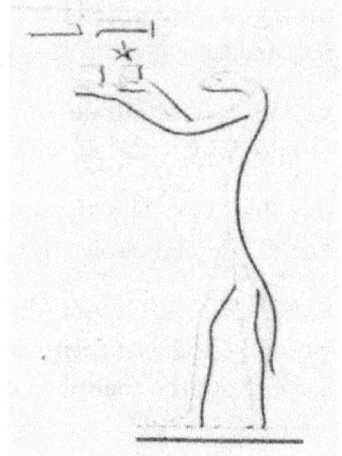

Egyptian name:

Tepy-Akhw (*tpy-ꜥꜣḫw*)

"Head of the spirits or ghosts"

Image:

Serpent with human legs, standing

Mineral:

Garnet and Gold

Aspect:

DAY 21: A. A. A. Do not go out on it on (any road on this day).

DAY 22: A. A. A. Anyone born on this day will not live. It is the day (of killing) the children of Bedesh (Apophis).

DAY 23: A. A. F. It is the day of offering... Abydos, (victuals)... invocation offering to the spirits (akhw).

DAY 24: A. A. A. (Do not mention the name of) Seth in (a loud voice) on this day. It is the day of (the rebellion) which he has done (against) Onnophris. As to anyone who mentions his name forgetfully, fighting (is made) in his house (for ever).

DAY 25: A. A. A. (Do not eat anything) which is on water. It is the day of cutting from the tongue of Sobek (in his Sethian aspect) on this day.

DAY 27: A. A. A. Do not go out of your house until Ra sets because the Majesty of the goddess Sekhmet is angry in the land of Temhu. Behold she went about, walking and standing (or, waiting) ...

DAY 28: F. F. F. If you see anything [in the sky], it will be good on this day.

DAY 29: F. F. F. The gods are satisfied (when) they give adoration to Onnophris, incense being on the fire, and your local gods... myrrh... pleasant on (this day).

LAST DAY: F. F. F. Offer to... Ptah-Sokar-Osiris... Atum, lord of the two lands (of Heliopolis)... to all the gods... on this day.

Abramelin:

Kolani, Kibigili, Corocana, Hipogo, Agikus,

Nagar, Echagi, Parachmo, Kosirma, Dagio

24. Baba.

24. BABA

(25th Decan)
Shemu month 1.1
harvest season
1st trimester (circa. March)

Egyptian name:
Akhw (*3ḫw*)

Image:
Human headed God

Mineral:
Gold

Aspect:
House of Ra (tomorrow)
House of Osiris (yesterday)
House of Horus (today)

DAY 1: F. F. F. (Feast of Horus), (son of) Isis and his followers … day …

DAY 2: A. A. A. Do not (sail ?) in any wind on this day.

DAY 3: F. F. F. If (you see any) thing, (it will be good on this day).

DAY 4: A. A. A. (Do not go out) of your house (on any) road on this day. It is the day of… year. Follow Horus on this day.

DAY 5: A. A. A. Feast of Ba-neb-djedet (on this day) …(As to any who goes out of his house on this day, disease abandons him until) he dies.

DAY 6: F. F. F. Coming of the great ones from the House of Ra rejoicing on this day when they receive the Wedjat-eye together with their followers. If you see anything, it will be good on this day.

DAY 7: F. F. F. The crew follow Horus in the foreign land, examining its list therein when he smote him who rebelled against his master. Every land is happy, and their heart is glad ...

DAY 8: (NO SPACE). If you see anything, it will be good on this day.*

DAY 9: F. F. F. If you see anything [in the sky], it will be good on this day ... Ennead.

DAY 10: A. A. A. Proceeding of the white one (Hathor) of heaven upstream to seek at the front among (those who rebelled against their) master in the Delta.

Abramelin:
Oromonas, Hagos, Mimosah, Arakuson, Rimog, Iserag, Cheikaseph, Kofan, Batirunos, Cochaly,

25. Khent-ḥeru

---

* substituted the missing section in Cairo mss from British Museum mss

(26TH DECAN)
SHEMU MONTH I
HARVEST SEASON
2ND TRIMESTER
(CIRCA. MAR - APR)

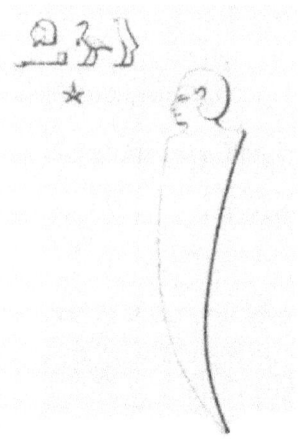

Egyptian name:

Tepy bawey (*tpy3 bʿw(y)*)

Image:

Human-headed, armless God with body ending in a crocodile's tail. Its name literally "head or herald of the twin souls", which is next decan, and a very strange one.

Mineral:

Gold

Aspect:

DAY 11: found missing. . . (in his attendance). . . Holy House (*ḥwt-ḏsrt*).

DAY 12: A. A..A Do not. ... he goes forth . . his body. . .

DAY 13: . . . F. ... Do not. . . to (or, until).

DAY 14: A. A. A. . . . Apophis in. . . cutting into (or, from) (the tongue of the enemy of) Sobek (on this day). It is the day of. . . his head by. . .

DAY 15: A. A. A. (Any one born on this day) he will die. . . Do not go out of your house until Ra sets) in the horizon. . .

DAY 16: F. ...F (you see anything on this day). . .

DAY 17: (If) you see anything, it will be good (on this day). . . The Ennead is in joy and the crew (of Ra) is in festivity.

DAY 18: missing

DAY 19: F. F. F. It is the day of counting in the presence of (?) by Thoth who heard Maat, this great one. All gods are in great festivity.

DAY 20: A. A. A. Maat judges in front of these gods who became angry in the island of the sanctuary of Letopolis. The Majesty of Horus revised it.

Abramelin:

Ienuri, Nephasser, Bekaro, Hyla, Eneki,

Maggio, Abbetira, Breffeo, Ornion, Schaluach,

26. Ḥer-áb-khentu.

26. Ḥer-áb-khentu.

(27th Decan)
Shemu month I
harvest season
3rd trimester (circa. April)

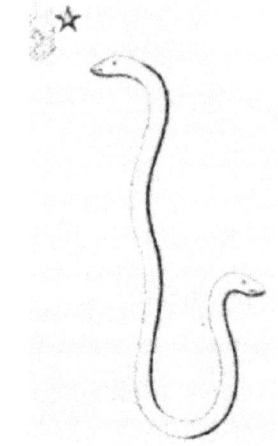

Egyptian name:

Baw(y) (*bʿw(y)*) (The twin Bas)

Image:

Erect serpent with up-curved tail

Mineral:

Gold and unknown substance connected with horses (and perhaps dogs)*

Aspect:

DAY 21: A. A. A. Vomiting the things which come back from the boat, so that no follower of Ra remains, namely, his followers (who are) in his attendance.

DAY 22: F. F. F. Anyone born on this day will die in old age . . .

DAY 23: F. F. F. If you see anything, (it will be good on this day).

DAY 24: A. A. A.† words of (?) the rebels ...

DAY 25: on this day ......

DAY 26: F. F. F. If you see anything, it will be good on this day).

DAY 27: A. A. A. . . Babai. . . (in) front of Ra. . .

DAY 28: F. F. F. . . . great. . . him on this day. . .

DAY 29: F. F. F.† If you see anything, (it will be good on this day). . .

---

* *tsmd/śsmit*

† substituted the missing section in Cairo mss from British Museum mss

(LAST DAY) : F. F. F. Feast of... happy.

Abramelin:

Hillaro, Ybario, Altono, Armefia, Belifares,
Camalo, Corilon, Dirilisin, Eralicarison, Elipinon,

27. Khent-kheru.

27. KHENT-KHERU . .

(28th Decan)
Shemu month 2
harvest season
1st trimester (circa. April)

Egyptian name:

Hor tep nefer (*ḥr tp nfr*)

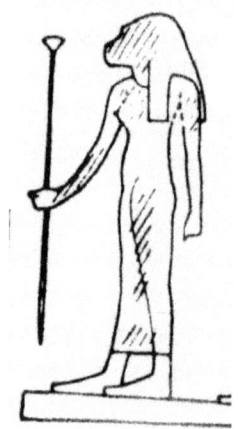

Image:

Lion-headed Goddess, standing with scepter and ankh

Mineral:

Gold

Aspect:

House of Ra (tomorrow)

House of Osiris (yesterday)

House of Horus (today)

DAY 1: F. F. F. ...... Osiris ...... gods(?)

DAY 2: [MISSING] Oh heart of the gods, listen very well—FOUND MISSING. The crew of Ra is in festivity.

DAY 3: F. F. F. The month of the followers of Ra. A day is fixed in heaven and on earth as a feast.

DAY 4: A. A. A. Do not shout at anybody on this day while that which Geb and Nut have done is counted in the presence (lit. on the hands) of the gods.

DAY 5: F. F. F. If you see anything, it will be good on this day.

DAY 6: F. F. F.* Horus proceeds to repel what was done against his father and to inquire from the followers of his father Onnophris on this day.

DAY 7: A. A. A. Do not go out of your house during waking-time... Ra in the horizon. It is the day of the executioners of Sekhmet. (counting) by names.

DAY 8: F. F. F. Make a holiday for Ra and his followers make a good day on this day.

DAY 9: F. F. F. Make incense of (different kinds of) sweet herbs for his followers (while pleasing) him on this day.

DAY 10: F. F. F. Anyone (born) on this day (he) will be noble.

Abramelin:

Gariniranus, Sipillipis, Ergomion, Lotifar, Chimirgu,

Kaerlesa, Nadele, Baalto, Ygarimi, Akahimo,

28. Qeṯ.

28. Qeṯ . . . . .

---

* Substituted the missing section in Cairo mss from British Museum mss

(29th decan)
Shemu month 2
harvest season
2nd lunar trimester
(circa. apr - may)

Egyptian name:

Khenetew kherew (ẖnt(w) ẖr(w))

Image:

Figure squatting on a plinth wearing white crown of lower Egypt. Or sometime described as Falcon headed God, standing offering two nw-jars, a duplicate of decan 32.

Mineral:

Red Jasper and Gold

Aspect:

DAY 11: A. A. A. Do not sail in a boat on the river. It is the day of catching birds and fish (by) the followers of Ra. (Anyone who sails) on the river he will not live.

DAY 12: F. F. F. If you see anything, it will be good on this day.

DAY 13: F. F. F. Feast of Wedjat in (settlement of) Dep, and her followers are (also) in festival when singing and chanting take place on the day of offering the incense (and all kinds of sweet herbs).

DAY 14: F. F. F. If you see anything, it will be good on this day.

DAY 15: A. A. A. Do not judge yourself... On this day. It is the day of fighting... their rebellion.

DAY 16: F. F. F. Anyone born on this day he will die great as a magistrate among all people.

DAY 17: A. A. A. Do not go out on it. Do not do anything, or any work on this day.

DAY 18: A. A. A. Do not eat the meat of any lion. It is the day of the going forth of Khenti (Osiris) of the god's house when he goes about to the holy mountain. All those who will smell death and skin rash will not recover.

DAY 19: A. A. A. The Ennead sails, they are much (i.e. numerous sailings of the Ennead) in the entire land. If any lion is seen, he will pass away at once. It is the day of judging the great ones on this day.

DAY 20: A. A. A. Many die when they come with adverse wind. Do not go out with any wind on this day.

Abramelin:

Golopa, Naniroa, Istaroth, Tedea, Ikon,

Kama, Arisaka, Bileka, Yromus, Camarion,

29. Sasaqeṭ.

29. SASAQEṬ . . . .

(30st Decan)
Shemu month 2
HARVEST SEASON
3RD LUNAR TRIMESTER (CIRCA. MAY)

Egyptian name:

Sa ked (*s3 ḳd*) "The Potter's Son"

Image:

Serpent with human arms, sometimes legs, standing, offering two nw-jars.

Mineral:

Glass and Gold

Aspect:

DAY 21: A. A. F. It is the day of the (decan) the Leg (w'rty) the children of Nut (epagomenal days). Do not go out on it until day-break (i.e. the ninth hour).

DAY 22: A. A. A. Disturbance below and uproar of the gods of the *kri-*shrines on this day when Shu was complaining (?) to Ra about the great ones of infinity. Do not go out on it.

DAY 23: F. F. F. The crew rest when they see the enemy of their master.

DAY 24: F. F. F. If you see anything [in the sky], (it will be) good on this day.

DAY 25: F. F. F. Pacified are the Akhet-eye, everything and everybody. It is pleasant to the gods and Ra.

DAY 26: A. A. A. The going forth of Neith. She treads on this day in the flood (in order to) look for things of Sobek. If any lion sees them, he will pass away immediately.

DAY 27: A. A. A. The cutting of the heads and the tying of the throats and the occurrence of the flight among the gods on this day. Do not (do) any work on this day.

DAY 28: F. F. F. Purifying things and offerings in Busiris. The gods spend the day in festivity. Act in accordance with that which happens (i.e. the event) on this day.

DAY 29: F. F. F. If you see anything, it will be good on this day.

LAST DAY: F. F. F. The going forth of Shu with the intention to bring back the Wedjat-eye, and appeasing Thoth on this day.

Abramelin:
Jamaih, Aragor, Igakis, Olaski, Haiamon,
Semechle, Alosom, Segosel, Boreb, Ugolog,

30. Ārt.

30. Ārt

(31st Decan)
Shemu month 3
harvest season
1st lunar trimester
(circa. May)

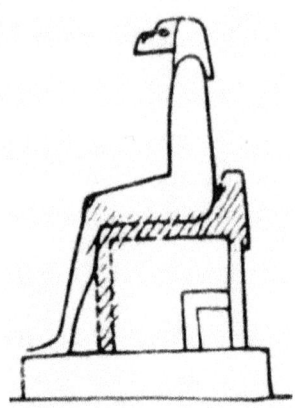

Egyptian name:

Khaw (ḫ3w) ("flowers - blue lily")

Image:

Lion-headed Goddess, mummified, seated.

Mineral:

Carnelian and Gold

Aspect:

House of Ra (tomorrow)

House of Osiris (yesterday)

House of Horus (today)

DAY 1: F. F. F. A great feast in the southern heaven, every land and everybody start jubilating. The mistress of heaven, *Ipt-ḥmt* (Hippo) *and* every land are in festivity on this day.

DAY 2: F. F. F. Every god and every goddess spend the day in festivity and in great astonishment in the sacred temple.

DAY 3: A. A. A. Anger of the divine-Majesty. Do not do anything on this day.

DAY 4: F. F. F. If you see anything, it will be good on this day.

DAY 5: A. A. A. Do not go out of your house. Do not proceed on a boat. Do not do any work on it. It is the day of the departure of this goddess to the place wherefrom she came. The heart of the gods is sad about them very much.

DAY 6: A. A. A. Do not fight or make uproar. . . in your house while every temple of the goddess is in (or like) this manner.

DAY 7: A. A. A. Sailing of the gods after the Majesty of the goddess. As for. . . on (or, in) it. . . A flame which takes place in front of everybody on this day.

DAY 8: A. A. A. Do not beat anybody. Do not strike anybody. It is the day of the massacre of the followers of the Majesty of the goddess.

DAY 9: F. F. F. The gods are content and they are happy because Ra is at peace with the Akhet-eye. Every god is in festivity on this day.

DAY 10: A. A. A. Creating enmity according to the event. The gods who are in the shrine, their hearts are sad.

Abramelin:
Hadcu, Amalomi, Bilifo, Granona, Pagalusta, Hyrmiua, Canali, Radina, Gezero, Sarsiee.

31. Khau.

31. Khau . . . . .

(32ND DECAN)
SHEMU MONTH 3
HARVEST SEASON
2ND LUNAR TRIMESTER
(CIRCA. MAY - JUN)

Egyptian name:

Aret (rt) "The Hawk's jaw or Beak"

Image:

Falcon headed God,
standing offering two nw-jars

Mineral:

Granite and Gold

Aspect:

DAY 11: A. A. A. Introducing the great ones by Ra to the booth to see what he had observed through the eye of Horus the Elder. They were with heads bent down when they saw an eye of Horus being angry in front of Ra. Do not perform any ritual on this day.

DAY 12: F. F. F. Holiday... Reception of Ra, (his) followers are in festivity, and everybody is in festivity.

DAY 13 : A. A. A. The Majesty of this god proceeds sailing westwards to see the beauty of Onnophris on this day.

DAY 14 : A. A. A. Do not burn on this day in your house with anything (in the way) of burning flame with any of its glow on that day of the anger of that eye of Horus the Elder.

DAY 15: F. F. F. If you see anything, it will be good. Horus hears your words in the presence of every god and every goddess on this day. You will see every good thing in your house.

DAY 16: A. A. A. It is the day of transmitting Maat to the shrine by the Majesty of Ra in the Heliopolis of Ra. These gods learnt that she was much blamed for it.

DAY 17: A. A. A. The escape of the fugitive (eye)... and the gods became deprived of Ra who had come to hand over the rebels to him ... in their path.

DAY 18: A. A. A. Do not go out of your house on any road on this day. The going forth of Maat and Ra... secret on this day. If anyone... outside... this trampling of a bull ...

DAY 19: A. A. A. Do not 'shake hands' on this day nor do any work on this day. Breaking of... into (or, through) water on this day.

DAY 20: A. A. A. Do not go out of your house on any road on this day.

Abramelin:

Soesman, Tmiti, Balachman, Gagison, Mafalach,

Zagol, Ichdison, Sumuram, Aglasis, Hachamel,

32. Ḳemen-ḥeru-àn-Saḥ.

32. Remen-ḥeru-an-Saḥ

(33rd Decan)
Shemu Month 3
Harvest Season
3rd Trimester (circa. June)

Egyptian name:

Remen hery (*rmn ḥry*)

Image:

Serpent with human arms and legs, offering two nw-jars

Mineral:

Quartz and Gold

Aspect:

DAY 21: F. F. F. If you see anything [in the sky], it will be good on this day.

DAY 22: A. A. A. Do not see any digging, any skin-rash or any fever on this day. It is the day of Sepa in Tura coming from Heliopolis.

DAY 23: A. A. A. Anyone born on this day will not live. It is the day of quarrelling and reproaching with Onnophris on this day.

DAY 24: F. F. F. It is the day of... children of Bedesh (Apophis). The gods killed them when he came. Then he sailed to the south.

DAY 25: F. A. F. Do not go out at midday; the great enemy (Apophis) is in the temple of Sekhmet.

DAY 26: F. F. F. If you see anything, it will be good on this day.

DAY 27: A. A. A. Do not go out of your house on this day. It is the day of sailing on the river, and of overthrowing the enclosure wall.

DAY 28: A. A. A. Creating misery, and bringing terror into existence in conformity with the custom of what is in the year.

DAY 29: F. F. F. The feast of Mut in Shera (the sacred lake at Karnak) on this day. It is the day of feeding the gods and her followers on this day.

LAST DAY: F. F. F. If you see anything [in the sky], it will be good on this day.

Abramelin:

Agasoly, Kiliosa, Ebaron, Zalones, Jugula,
Carahami, Kaflesi, Mennolika, Takarosa, Astolitu,

33. Mestcher-Saḥ.

33. Mestcher-Saḥ . .

(34RD DECAN)
SHEMU MONTH 4
HARVEST SEASON
1ST TRIMESTER (CIRCA. JUNE)

Egyptian name:
Tjes arek (*ts ʿrk*) "Maker of Knots"
A very old name for a magician

Image:
Lion-headed Goddess, seated with sistrum and flagellum

Mineral: Glass and Gold

Aspect:
House of Ra (tomorrow)
House of Osiris (yesterday)
House of Horus (today)

DAY 1: F. F. F. Transmitting the Great (*3ʿbt*) offerings (to) those who are in heaven. Every god and every goddess spend the day in the feast of Onnophris on this day.

DAY 2: F. F. F. Truth... (and all gods) perform the rites as one who is in heaven (i.e. Onnophris) day

---

*   Performing magic by weaving of spells in knots dates back to antiquity. The Egyptian word 'Heka' meaning magick, contains the hieroglyph of a knotted rope. al-Mu'awwidhatayn (seeking refuge) refers to last two sura of Koran, commonly used as amulets against 'blowers of knots' ie magicians.

DAY 3: A. A. A. (Proceeding of the Majesty of this goddess) to Heliopolis of Ra. A (feast) was made (on this day). Do not go out in order to do anything on this day.

DAY 4: A. A. F. It is the day of the procession of Sopdu (Sirius) together with his followers, being in a state of youth and remaining in the course of the day. Never will she be able to find a living soul.

DAY 5: F. F. F. 'Letopolis' (Maner) is in festivity, Min being at Akhmim. If you see anything, it will be good on this day.

DAY 6: A. A. A. Transmitting the rejuvenated one in Restau and hiding (the mysteries) of the conspirators on this day. (Do not do) anything on this day.

DAY 7: A. A. A. The dead one goes about in the necropolis and comes on earth. As to him who approaches him, he will suffer from the trampling of a bull and will not recover until he dies.

DAY 8: F. F. F. If you see anything, it will be good on this day.

DAY 9: F. F. F. Anyone born on this day will have noble honour.

DAY 10: F. F. F. It is the repulsion of the crew who was (in) the Delta. It is the day of the entering of the eye of Ra into his horizon when he sees his beauty.

Abramelin:
Merki, Anadi, Ekore,
Rosora, Negani,
Cigila, Secabmi, Calamos,
Sibolas, Forfasan,

34. Remen-kher-Saḥ.

34. Remen-kher-Saḥ.

(35RD DECAN)
SHEMU MONTH 4.2
HARVEST SEASON
2ND TRIMESTER (CIRCA. JUN - JUL)

Egyptian name:

Waret heret (wʿrt (hrt)) "Swift Peace".

Image:

Crocodile-headed God offering two nw-jars

Mineral:

Gold

Aspect:

DAY 11: A. A. A. Causing disturbance in the presence of the followers of Ra, and repelling the confederates of Seth into the eastern country.

DAY 12: F. F. F. Jubilation throughout the entire land on this day. The heart of those who are in the shrine is happy.

DAY 13: F. F. F. A holiday because of defending the son of Osiris... back of the portal by Seth.

DAY 14: F. F. F. Establishing her seat and hall... god portal (on the) first (occasion) on this day.

DAY 15: A. A. A. Do not do (any) thing. Do not go out on any road on this day... going forth of Ra to, propitiate Nun... in his cavern (in front of) his followers and the Ennead of the mesektet-barque on this day

DAY 16: F. F. F... to give water to those who are (in) the underworld Ennead of the west. It is pleasant to your father and your mother who are in the necropolis.

DAY 17: F. F. F. If you see anything, it will be good on this day.

DAY 18: A. A. F. Do not go out at the time of the morning because of the crew who leads (or, is leading) the rebels. If any lion goes out on earth on this day (he) will be blind, and they will say: he will not live.

DAY 19: F. F. F. Celebrate your feast of your god. Appease your spirit (akh), for this Eye of Horus has returned complete, nothing is missing in it.

DAY 20: A. A. A. Do not kill a guardian serpent on this day. It is the day of the cleaning and revision of the noble ones. There is silence because of it on earth in order to propitiate the Wedjat-eye on this day.

Abramelin:

Andrachor, Notiser, Filakon, Horasul, Saris,

Ekorim, Nelion, Ylemis, Calacha, Sapasani,

35. Ā-Saḥ.

(36th decan)
Shemu month 4
Harvest season
3rd trimester (circa. July)

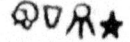

Egyptian name:

Tepy-aspedet (*tpy-ʿspdt*)

"The one who comes before Sirius"*

Image:

Erect serpent with human arms,
offering two nw-jars

Mineral:

Ebony and Gold

Aspect:

DAY 21: F. F. F. If you see anything, it will be good on this day.

DAY 22: F. F. F. The feast of Anubis who is on his mountain on this day. The children of [Geb] and Nut spend the day in festivity, which is a holiday after the good bath of the gods on this day.

DAY 23: A. A. A. Do not taste bread or beer on this day because the... of that which was done before him who rebelled against his master on this day.

DAY 24: F. F. F. Make Great (*3ʿbt*) offerings to the gods in the presence of Ra. Make a holiday in your house.

---

* A reference to the famous event, the heliacal rising of Sirius, which must once have occured near the solstice but due to the phenomenon of precession, has move back further into the year and these days occurs in late August.

DAY 25: F. F. F. The god is ... established in front of the crew of Ra who is happy in the Holy House (*ḥwt-dsrt*).

DAY 26: F. A. F. Do not go out on it at midday. The gods . . . (sail) with all winds. . . takes place. . . (Do not) go out of your house

DAY 27: A. A. A. . . . earth. Do not do anything on it.

DAY 28: F. F. F. . . . (Feast) on Min. Day of. . . If (you see anything), it will be good on this day.

DAY 29: F. F. F. .. Holiday in the temple of Sokar, in the estate of Ptah, and those who are in this estate are in great festivity, being healthy.

LAST DAY: F. F. F. .. Anything which comes forth on it in the estate of Ptah will be good. As for anything (or, offering), any rite or anybody on this day, it is good throughout the year. Sing and offer much.

Abramelin:

Seneol, Charonthona, Carona, Regerio, Megalogi,
Irmana, Elami, Ramgisa, Sirigilis, Boria.

36. Saḥ.

36. SAḤ . . . . .

The Five (Unlucky) days - Spells of protection & propitiation

In a lunar calendar we have been using there is no need for the additional days on the year one finds in the so-called Civic solar calendar, the 360+5 variety that was prominent in pharaonic times. Nevertheless, they are of interest because they come with magical spells to avert the dangers of the times, especially so on these five extra or unlucky days. They could be part of a group of spells whose purpose was to counteract the malign influence of certain times. So we can use them to counter the adverse influences of some of the days within each decan. Here they are:

The great ones are born. As for the great ones whose forms are not mysterious, beware of them. Their occasion (or, deeds) will not come. . . They have proceeded (thus):

BIRTH OF OSIRIS,

BIRTH OF HAROERIS (THE ELDER HORUS),

BIRTH OF SETH,

BIRTH OF ISIS,

BIRTH OF NEPHTHYS.

AS TO ANYONE WHO KNOWS THE NAME OF THE FIVE EPAGOMENAL DAYS, he does not hunger, he does not thirst, Bastet does not overpower him. He will not enter into the great law court, he will not die through an enemy of the king and will not die (or, depart) through the pestilence of the year. But he will last every day (till) death arrives, whereas no illness will take possession of him.

AS TO HIM WHO KNOWS THEM, *Hw* will be prosperous within him, his speech is important to listen to in the presence of Ra.

FIRST DAY : THE BIRTH OF OSIRIS. WORDS TO BE SAID ON IT:

O Osiris, bull in his cavern (whose) name is hidden ... offspring (?) of his mother. Hail to thee, hail to thee (??). I am (thy son)... O father, Osiris.

THE NAME OF THIS DAY: The pure one, field

SECOND DAY : THE BIRTH OF HORUS. WORDS TO BE SAID ON IT :

O Horus, (*khenty-irty*) of Letopolis. It is repeated anew mighty of strength, master of fear, save me from bad and evil things and from any slaughter. Horus, son of Geb

THE NAME OF THIS DAY: powerful is the heart

THIRD DAY : THE BIRTH OF SETH. WORDS TO BE SAID ON IT:

OH, SETH, Son of Nut, great of strength, save me from bad and evil things and from any slaughter, protection is at thy hands of thy holiness. I am the son of thy son.

THE NAME OF THE DAY : It is powerful of heart.

FOURTH DAY : THE BIRTH OF ISIS. WORDS TO BE SAID ON IT:

Oh, this Isis, daughter of Nut the eldest, mistress of magic, provider (?) of the book, mistress who appeases the two lands, her face is glorious. I am the brother and the sister.

THE NAME OF THE DAY : He who makes terror.

FIFTH DAY : THE BIRTH OF NEPHTHYS. WORDS TO BE SAID ON IT :

Oh, Nephthys, daughter of Nut, sister of Seth, she whose father sees a healthy daughter, beautiful of face. Beautiful of face. I am the divine power in the womb of my mother Nut.

THE NAME OF THE DAY: The child who is in his nest.

WORDS TO BE SAID AFTER THEM WHEN THE EPAGOMENAL DAYS (OR UNLUCKY DAYS) ARE COMPLETED.

Hail to you! O great ones according to their names, children of a goddess who have come forth from the sacred womb, lords because of their father, goddesses because of their mother, without knowing the necropolis. Behold, may you protect (me) and save me. May you make me prosperous, may you make protection, may you repeat and may you protect me. I am one who is on their list.

THIS SPELL IS TO BE SAID FOUR TIMES.

Make for thyself an amulet as protection, [drawn on fine linen] and placed about the neck (for the five) epagomenal days in (the name of) these gods on the day. . . written on the choice of. . . amulet. . .THE FEMALE FIGURE of Isis, THE FEMALE FIGURE of Nephthys . . . BLACK COLOUR ANOINTED WITH FIRST CLASS OIL AND FUMIGATED WITH INCENSE ON A BURNER. THEY SHOULD BE PURIFIED, LOOSENED, AND THROWN INTO WATER for the father Nun and for the mother Nut after the day of the birth of Ra and act. Behold, make for thyself a big *3ᶜbt* (offering) of bread, beer, oxen, fowl, carob beans incense *ty-sps-wood* and all kinds of dates and vegetables — being clean, being clean in front of Ra-Harakhti when he shines in the eastern horizon of heaven and when he sets in the western horizon. Behold, thou bathest in the fresh water ... of the beginning of inundation. Paint thine eyes with green paint; take a drink of wine and anoint thyself...

The Demonic Calendar After the Pharaohs

The Demonic Calendar Ancient Egypt, the title of this book, in which I have compiled all the available data to be had about the 10 day weeks or calendrical system of pharaonic Egypt. This survives in talismanic magick as well as in the decans of astrology. It was assumed that the Egyptian hadn't regularised the decans (which originally only had calendrical function) but this is exactly what the mathematically orientated Greeks did for them.

But looking deeper it seems these Egyptian decans were connected with what they called a person's trifold "soul", a mysterious mix of the Ba, the Ka and the Akh. Think of it as a guardian spirit, or demon, that became associated with someone at birth. So using all these sources, we can try to identify and analyze this demon that influences a person's inner being from birth.

DECANS OF WESTERN ASTROLOGY
THEIR MEANING

This system of decans did not fall out of use after the fall of Egypt, there are several derived versions, including one popular in South Asia.[1] where it was said that "Thirty-six are the thirds of the zodiacal signs, which are called Drekinas by the Greeks. They have various clothes, forms,

---

1. Yavanajātaka of Sphujidhvaja, translated by David Pingree published as "The India Iconography of the Decans and Horâs" in Journal of the Warburg and Courtauld Institutes, Vol. 26, No. 3/4 (1963), pp. 223-254

and colours; I will describe them with all their qualities beginning with their characteristic signs."

These solar decans, based on the ecliptic and the zodiac. I gave the native Egyptian description in chapter two, although the descriptions are very terse, and the reader is invited to supplement this with the following compilation of the more detailed interpretations that come to us in the modern era via several convoluted routes.

The Indian version is a rendering of what turns out to be a Greek version popular in the classical world. Like many magical ideas, these were later translated into Arabic for use by Muslims and Sufis and it is from the Islamic world that they come to the west. For some time now I've been promulgating an east-west version of magick, one that assumes there is a multinational pool of ideas, common to Egypt, India and the West; this text seems to be an obvious example of such a tradition. Or in a nutshell, what goes around comes around, is definitely true of magick.

A Case Study

THOUGHTS ON INTERPRETATION

The reader will no doubt be aware that western zodiac has at least two versions, the so-called tropical or virtual zodiac which is a notional band that doesn't quite coincide with the corresponding constellations due to a phenomenon known as precession. The actual position of the constellations has moved by more than 30degrees in the 2000 odd years since it was codified in Greek astronomy. Modern astrological systems can make use of either the tropical or the sidereal zodiac.

So for example, someone commonly referred to as sun sign Pisces in the tropical zodiacs, could be reframed in the sidereal zodiacs by simple expedient of adding six degrees and subtracting a sign. So a Piscean in one system would be an Aquarian in the sidereal system. So, in terms of decans, which should one read? My solution, based on some experience, is to read both. The tropical as the more manifest you, and alongside this the sidereal as a counterpoint, the hidden you if you like.

So take an imaginary person born on 19th March 1961. Born at around 4pm.

So looking back at the calendar we find that this person was born under the first decan of the lunar month, which in the traditional listing is decan 25., the 3rd day of the 10 day sequence, second part. So, from Egypian point of view this would be the 3rd day of 25th decan, latter part.

For many, knowing the traditional birth demon is important for all sorts of reasons, including the belief that this entity is synonymous with one's guardian spirit or daemon, an important influence to understand and one which is said to be closest on one's birthday. So one begins by looking at the most ancient Egyptian records for this subject, which are given on page 98 above.

We see this is called *Akhw*, which is the nearest one can get to the word Daemon in the old Egyptian tongue. So important is this entity that my book Supernatural Assault in Ancient Egypt is almost devoted to this topic. They are, in effect, the archetype for all such demonic things.

It is also pleasing to read that anyone born on this day will have a favourable day, and whatever omens they see, will be good and favourable.

It has to be said that the Egyptian records that we have are a bit terse and leave a lot to the imagination. Luckily we can now supplement this with material from after the pharaohs, when these ideas were passed on and supplemented.

In later versions of this system, the decans are given, mapped or transferred to the Near Eastern Zodiac which, familiar to us from Western astrology. Thus we look at the Third Decan of Pisces.

The constellation assigned to this decan is Andromeda, which has an interesting mythology. We should also note the similarity to the Night demon Andromalius, in the corresponding section of *Goetia*.

Our next stop after the pharaonic material is the *Testament of Solomon*, an ancient magical book that details the magical techniques ascribed to the famous sorcerer king. In reality, this seems to be a work dated to sometime after the first century of the common era and rich in Egyptian magical lore. At one stage in the narrative Solomon summons the decanal demons and asks them their name and function. The thirty-sixth said: "I am called Bianakith. I have a grudge against the body. I lay waste houses, I cause flesh to decay, and all else that is similar. If a man writes on the front-door of his house: 'Mêltô, Ardu, Anaath,' I will flee from that place."

From this, the demonic nature of the decans is confirmed along with their ambiguous nature, both cause illness but also indicating a remedy. In this case the subject may be subject to infections and should take the necessary precautions. This demon, like the Egyptian Akhw, is also particularly associated with the home, as a domestic spirit, and some care should be taken in the home, for instance honouring ancestral spirits and departed relatives.

This seems a good point to take account of the ruling planet said to be Mars, the various archetypes of which seem to recur in the remaining indicators.

The next thing to note is the formation from another ancient magical book known to us as the *Goetia*, or *Lesser Key of Solomon*. Though compiled in the 1600s, its sources seem much older. The Goetia has 72 spirits, who can be divided into two groups of 36, one for the day, and other for the night. The night demon is Andromalius, which is described as a man carrying a great serpent. In this system, serpent imagery abounds, sometimes positive, sometimes not so. We might say this is a good omen, and denotes that one will receive wisdom, represented by the serpent, from a distinctive person.

Next look at the Yavana Jataka (YJ), a text extant in India but whose title means something like Greek Nativities. The text itself follows the Egyptian system, and after the Islamic period in India, its idea passed back to the Middle East and from there to Byzantium and the West. In it we read that "The third Decan in Pisces is a woman whose hair has been loosened and who wears ornaments bearing the emblem of (the tribe of) abhiiras (cow?).* Ahirs or Yudav tribe of nomadic herdsmen, same lineage as Krishna) She shrieks, as she is frightened. She stands in the water adorned by troops of spirits having the shapes of jackals, cats, and boars."

The loosened hair seems the key image here, letting one's hair down says it all, so this is the wild, party animal side of one's personality. Also something tribal and ancestral, the other side of the tracks.

Then we turn to the latest recension of the text which surfaces in 1100s in writings of Jewish scholar Abraham Ibn Ezra or Even Ezra, which was repacked several times until translated into English in the 1655 edition of the celebrated astrologer William Lilly, which he called *The Astrological Optics* In this there is quite a lot of information: "The third face is of Mars and is a face of fornication and embraces of great delight with women and loving peace and quietness. The third is a young man embracing a beautiful woman." Which has much the same vibe as the earlier Indian text. This also provides oracles for each day of the ten, hence for day 23, it describes "A woman swimming in a boat," said to "denotes an inconstant person." – which in modern parlance we might view as, again, the scarlet woman, or one who has let her hair down somewhat.

The modern divinatory tarot deck also contains material to do with the decans, hidden in the small numbered cared, 2-10 in four suits, $4 \times 9 = 36$

So, in this case we turn to the interpretation of the 10 Cups where the following was assembled from unknown occult sources by historian Arthur Waite:

Appearance of Cups in a rainbow; it is contemplated in wonder and ecstasy by a man and woman below, evidently husband and wife. His right arm is about her; his left is raised upward; she raises her right arm. The two children dancing near them have not observed the prodigy but are happy after their own manner. There is a home-scene beyond.

Divinatory Meanings: Contentment, repose of the entire heart; the perfection of that state; also perfection of human love and friendship; if with several picture-cards, a person who is taking charge of the Querent's interests; also the town, village or country inhabited by the Querent. Reversed: Repose of the false heart, indignation, violence. This last meaning is closest to the meanings given earlier.

Finally then we can consider the esoteric meanings of the element of water which is attributed to this decan. This is very general and will apply to several decans and will itself be water of different types, perhaps Martian water.

"Water reflects, dissolves, washes away helps growth. The sea has plumbable depths and holds much within it. It can be a calm exterior which can be deceptive since sudden storms blow up, and hidden undercurrents can drag down.

Water has no shape of its own. It takes on the shape of its container, Once contained iit can be calm and useful, but often damping. As a rushing torrent, it can be overwhelming and destructive, It has great carrying power and force if properly contained or canalised. This is best exemplified by the fixed sign scorpio.

Those with one or other of these signs prominent in their charts have a certain distrust of self. They need someone to reflect. They are happier when their fluidity is given shape by someone else, they are naturally sensitive and are the carriers of intuition and inspiration which they can express in such ways as rhythms of art or poetry, music, dancing or in the exercise of the psychic faculties. They are deep, emotional, secretive, protective.

They tend to dislike people who are boisterous or who have strong personalities, finding them turing. Water feels that fire will make it boil and air will make it evaporate, but earth will contain it.

Their faults can be that they are literally "unstable as water" , too easily being a reflection of the last persona they were with, too inclined to emotional storms, too ready to be a drag on others by subversive actions, too sensitive to influence. Slang words are aptly descriptive of the water nature: "sloppy" "wet" a wet blanket" a drip, No one is all water and the less desirable tendencies may be balanced elsewhere."

All of the above, "fire water" perhaps, so doubly intoxicating.

I'm just laying out the basic details in the order in which I looked at them. In practice, it takes about an hour to talk through all these aspects and explain their implications. So that's more than enough. But, as it happens, there is a second set that could be looked at based on the Sidereal zodiac, in which one adds approximately six days and subtracts a sign. A whole new horoscope appears. So whilst the decanal spirit represents a person's hidden counterpart, animus or anima. Which raises the question, what part of the soul is the sidereal self? Perhaps the super-ego, the hidden hidden depths of personality. I will leave it for the reader to explore this for themselves.

The remainder of this chapter is a compilation of all of this available data for all nativities:

28. The First decan of Aries

Constellation: Cepheus [2]

Planet: (Chaldean) Mars

Element: Fire[3]

We could be talking about a person born in this ten day period or perhaps an event linked with it. This is said to be dominated by the fire element, with all the things one might associate Ardent, Keen. and Positive. Mars, the traditional ruler of the sign, is said to be strong. So we might call this Martial fire, which can be aggression prone to violent outbursts.

As one might expect "All three fire signs, ie Aries, Leo & Sagittarius, have something in common. All three have something of the nature of fire which actively burns, crackles, consumes, warms, delights or annoys according to whether it is suitable or not. It is delightful in the hearth, obnoxious if causing damage where it should not be burning.

Hence in a person it makes them active, ardent, enthusiastic, aspiring, emotionally able to burn with excitement or feeling of any kind, to become noisy actually or metaphorically, to have strong appetites for life, to be overpowering in consuming their less forceful companions, to be inflamed with the warmth which they bring to any interest, to delight when not in

---

2. Frances Rolleston, *Mazzaroth* (Weiser Books: York Beach / ME, 2001). First published 1865. Using her order for constellations but correcting start point for Sirius according to the Esna B zodiac, see D Pingree *Hephaestion*, Neugebauer, O., and Richard A. Parker. *Egyptian Astronomical Texts*. 1960 vol3 pp168-172

3. Margaret Hone, *A Modern Textbook of Astrology*, Fowler 1975, p38 & pp53sq

congenial company, They tend to be impatient of more sensitive or gentler people , thinking them slow or damping. "fire" feels that "water will extinguish it, and "earth" will smother it, but that "air" will fan its flames.

They are cheerful, gay, fond of sport and the joy of easer pulsating life. Their possible faults are those of being too lively , often rushing rashly into over-excitable, over-vivid unthoughtful, hence harmful or destructive ways. But no one is all Fire, and such tendencies may be balanced elsewhere in a chart.

TAROT: 2 OF WANDS[4]

The traditional tarot also preserves some knowledge of the decans. Thus the first decan of Aries was said to correspond with the . The image is traditional but again its origins and antiquity is difficult to decide. Illustrated images of small cards of Tarot were apparently influenced by the 15th century Solabusca deck though they are not identical and it looks like Arthur Waite, who researched this in the early 20th century, drew upon published and unpublished occult traditions, which may preserve additional ancient lore.

In some ways, these interpretations of the decans in the tarot are some of the most accessible to the modern sensibility:

"A tall man looks from a battlemented roof over sea and shore; he holds a globe in his right hand, while a staff in his left rests on the battlement; another is fixed in a ring. The Rose and Cross and Lily should be noticed on the left side. Divinatory Meanings: Between the alternative readings there is no marriage possible; on the one hand, riches, fortune,

---

4 Waite, Arthur Edward. The Pictorial Key to the Tarot. Lond, 1911. Print.

magnificence; on the other, physical suffering, disease, chagrin, sadness, mortification. The design gives one suggestion; here is a lord overlooking his dominion and alternately contemplating a globe; it looks like the malady, the mortification, the sadness of Alexander amidst the grandeur of this world's wealth. Reversed: Surprise, wonder, enchantment, emotion, trouble, fear."

ASTROLOGICAL OPTICS (AO)[5]

Back a few centuries to the Carolingian renaissance and a source says "it is a face of Boldness, Fortitude, Stournesse, and Immodesty. In the First Face of Aries ascends a Valiant man, Armed, holding out a Faucion, [a curved sword], in his right hand.(AO)

YAVANA JATAKA (YJ)

An even earlier tradition known from India "The first Decan in Aries is a man garbed in red and having a red complexion, a fierce man whose limbs and hands are wounded and who attacks in anger. He bears golden mail and bright arrows, and his hand is raised with an axe."

THE GOETIA[6]

A popular magical book The Goetia has 72 spirits we can be allocated to the decans, ie

---

5. Astrological Optics is the English translation dated 1655 of John Angelus, a translation dated 1494 from Venice, of the work ascribed to the famous twelfth century Jewish scholar EvenEzra or Abraham ibn Ezra.
6. *The Goetia, Lesser Key of Solomon the King,* Translated by MacGregor Mathers, edited by Aleister Crowley, Weiser MA, 1995
7. The Testament of Solomon, translated by F. C. Conybeare. 1898, digital edition by Joseph H. Peterson, 1997.

(Day) Bael. Cat-Toad-Man
(Night) the avian Phoenix "with the voice of a Child.

TESTAMENT OF SOLOMON[7]

Even earlier is the Testament of Solomon which treats the decanal demons as disease entities, with an underlying disease theory. As well as the connection between these demons and certain diseases the texts offer a rudimentary counter measure. We know from Egyptian sources, that such spells would form only part of the remedy, and they would no doubt be applied in conjunction with a medicament or physical intervention:

"I, O Lord, am called Ruax, and I cause the heads of men to be idle, and I pillage their brows. But let me only hear the words, 'Michael, imprison Ruax,' and at once I retreat."

As in the Egyptian almanac published as The Cairo Calendar, each day of the decan also has a particular meaning attached to it, either as an indication of the character of a person born this day or as a simple omen for it. Where these images originate, is thus far, difficult to say but each day or degree appear as a slight variation on the element. Thus the first day of ten will be:

DAY BY DAY (AO)

1. A man holding a sickle in his right hand and in his left an engine of war, a man then born or querent shall be hardworking and much exercised in warlike affairs.
2. A man having a head like a dog, stretching out his right hand towards the skies and holding a staff in his left hand, denotes a litigious and troublesome person, as envious as a dog.
3. A handsome man, stretching forth his right hand as if he were showing the various things in the world, and applying his left hand to a girdle bound about him signifies a peaceable, quiet person.
4. A man with curled beard of hair, holding a hawk in his right hand

and a whip in his left signifies some seldom rich but a spender of his estate. Consuming all e hath in his age.

5. Two men, one holding in his hand an axe, cleaving wood, the other holding a scepter in his right hand, denote a provident housekeeper and a provider for his family.

6. A king crowned, holding a globe in his right hand and a scepter in his left. The native under this ascension will exceed all his kindred and acquaintances in greatness.

7. A man armed all over holding a dart in his right hand denotes a wary careful person, a preserver of himself.

8. A man having his head covered with a helmet and nowhere else armed holding in his right hand a crossbow signals a quarrelsome, contentious person and murderers

9. A man bare headed, well clothed over his body with a gown , holding a sword in his left hand , with the point downwards signifies a talkative person full of words and of a wonderful spirit.

10. A man, bare-headed, but clothed over his body, piercing a bear thro with a spear denotes a forester or hunter

29. Second decan of Aries

Constellation: Andromeda

Planet : Sun

Element: fire

Reread the section on fire from the previous decan as these will still be relevant here. But the fire has changed slightly to solar fire, which is the result of a nuclear reaction, so the visible fierce heat of the sun rather than the metaphorical fire of mars. Ultimately this is the source of all life, but too much of it and life is consumed.

Tarot: 3 wands

"A calm, stately personage, with his back turned, looking from a cliff's edge at ships passing over the sea. Three staves are planted in the ground, and he leans slightly on one of them. Divinatory Meanings: He symbolizes established strength, enterprise, effort, trade, commerce, discovery; those are his ships, bearing his merchandise, which are sailing over the sea. The card also signifies able co-operation in business, as if the successful merchant prince were looking from his side towards yours with a view to help you. Reversed: The end of troubles, suspension or cessation of adversity, toil and disappointment."

AO

"The second face of Aries is of the Sun, and is a face of Nobility, Highnesse, Rule, and Great Dominion. In the Second Face ascends a man in a gown like a Clergyman."

YJ

"Which is the second Decan in Aries is a pale-hued warrior whose eyes are pitiless to his enemies. He is clothed in white. His head is like an elephant's. He has arrows for weapons, and he knows the purposes of minerals and mercury. His limbs are heavy and hairy."

Goetia

(Day) An old man riding a crocodile carrying a goshawk;
(Night) "Stock dove with a sore throat"

Testament of Solomon:

"I am called Barsafael, and I cause those who are subject to my hour to feel the pain of migraine. If only I hear the words, 'Gabriel, imprison Barsafael,' at once I retreat."

Day by day:

11. A woman standing holding a distaff in her right hand signifies a person loving friendship and hospitality.
12. An eagle, spreading out her wings over her young ones, sitting under her denotes an ambitious person, proud.
13. A subtle person with his right hand holding a goat by the horns, denotes a wondrous famous person
14. A captive man standing upright between two pillars having his arms bound with two chains denotes a person much subject to imprisonment.
15. A man bare-headed, his arms stretched out and clothed with habergeon signifies thieves, reckless, lewd and wicked persons.
16. A man labouring with a dungfork or sometimes a man pouring water out of a pitcher denotes a fishman or a labourer.
17. A man standing idle clothed in sinc silk represents a fine delicate person
18. A woman sitting on a chair holding up her right hand denotes a man loving peace and quietness
19. A man clothed with a habergeon standing and showing treasure and money with his hands signifies a wicked, debauched person.

20. A man with a helmet on his head, and an ostrich feather in his hat, riding upon a bull, leading a horse with his left hand, a man born with this sign will be malicious

30. Third decan of Aries

Constellation: Casseopeia

Planet: (Chaldean) Venus

Element: Fire

The venusian variety. Venus is very close to the sun and the temperature on its surface is hot enough to melt lead. But this is still reflected fire, and therefore the fire of emotions that can turn something golden.

Tarot: 4 wands

"From the four great staves planted in the foreground there is a great garland suspended; two female figures uplift nosegays; at their side is a bridge over a moat, leading to an old manorial house. Divinatory Meanings: They are for once almost on the surface--country life, haven of refuge, a species of domestic harvest-home, repose, concord, harmony, prosperity, peace, and the perfected work of these. Reversed: The meaning remains unaltered; it is prosperity, increase, felicity, beauty, embellishment."

(AO)
"The Third Face of Aries is of Venus, and is a Face of Subtilty in every Work, and of Meekness, of Play, Mirth, and Beauty. The Third Face ascends like a young woman, sitting on a stool, and playing on a lute."

(YJ)
"The third Decan in Aries wears dark blue garments and has a dark blue body. Armed with a club, he is fierce. He has a garland of blue diadems. He is strong with leaps (?), and his eyeballs are like a bull's. He is like Death in battle."

THE GOETIA

(Day) Similar to previous An old man riding a crocodile carrying a goshawk; (Night) Crow with sore throat.

Testament of Solomon:

"I am called Arôtosael. I do harm to eyes, and grievously injure them. Only let me hear the words, 'Uriel, imprison Aratosael' (sic), at once I retreat . . . . ."

Day by Day (AO)

21. A dog sitting and turning his face towards a lion signifies a faithful companion
22. A bear sitting and holding a great beam in his mouth will be a wicked person.
23. Six serpents, three of them fighting against the other three signifies a man born with many enemies
24. A naked woman covers her secrets with her left hand and holding up her right hand, if the native be a woman she will be desirous of a man, if a man much given to women.
25. A man of curled locks, riding upon a ram, holding him by the horns signifies a citizen covetous to bear rule.
26. 2 suns one shining against the other, a man bearing rule and keeping his power, is signified hereby.
27. A great dragon lying upon the earth, a man who will be potent in his old age.
28. A woman standing upright, being well clothed signifies a pleasant peaceable person.
29. A man holding a saw in his hands, a laborious person nourishing himself and his wife by his labour.
30. An austere woman leading a saddled horse in her right hand. The native under this degree will be high minded , ambitious to bear rule over others.

31. First decan of Taurus

Constellation: Cetus

Planet: (Chaldean) Venus

Element: Earth

Again they are as the traditional name implies. From this comes the phrase "he is of the earth" The phrase "down to earth" is explanatory also "down to bedrock.

Earth is solid, dependable for support, motionless, dry, in modern idiom "functional" and rather uninteresting. No one is all "earth", but those in whose charts one or more of these signs are prominent have these traits of solid dependable, practicality. They are capable and hard working in sensible ways, either in actual building or the building of careers and organisations.

They are careful and trustworthy with possessions or finance and will look after the small matters which make the complete whole. They tend to be suspicious or dubious about more lively agile-minded people, thinking them disturbing and trivial.

Earth feels "air" will dry it, "fire will parch it but that water will refresh it.

Their faults are liable to be that in their customary applications to material ends, they lack knowledge of the more abstract and inspirational things of life and may be thought dull by livelier people. Their faults can be narrowness of outlook, and too close addictions to order and to routine. Certain expressions are indicative - "He's rather a clod." No one is all Earth and such tendencies may be balanced elsewhere in the chart.

Tarot: 5 pentacles

"Two mendicants in a snow-storm pass a lighted casement.

Divinatory Meanings: The card foretells material trouble above all, whether in the form illustrated--that is, destitution--or otherwise. For some cartomancists, it is a card of love and lovers-wife, husband, friend, mistress; also concordance, affinities. These alternatives cannot be harmonized. Reversed: Disorder, chaos, ruin, discord, profligacy."

(AO)

"The first face of Taurus, is the face of Mercury, and it is a face of plowing, sowing, building, peopling houses, of learning and wisdom in the earth, and of learning in geometry. The first face of Taurus, ascends or raises up a book, a young man tilling the ground"

(YJ)

"The first Decan in Taurus is a black woman, happy as her mind is agitated by sidelong glances (?). Round her neck she wears a garland full of kadamba-flowers. She shines forth holding an axe in her hand. Her body is bowed down to by cow-herds."

Goetia:

(Day) Samigina Little horse or ass.
(Night) Raum, Crow.

Testament of Solomon::

"I am called Iudal, and I bring about a block in the ears and deafness of hearing. If I hear, 'Uruel Iudal,' I at once retreat."

day by day(AO)

1. Ascendeth a man leaning a bull to the slaughter, holding a staff in his hand. It signifies a hangman

2. Arises a woman holden a horse tail in her hand, it denotes an idle person
3. ascends an old woman, naked, covering her pudenda with her left hand. It signifies a woman desirous of a man in her old age, and to continue young.
4. A woman holding a whip in her right hand, It denotes a hasty angry person
5. Ariseth a bull sitting in a cauldron. By this ascension are signified men, loving hospitality, good house keepers.
6. Ascends man having three heads, and pointing to the ground with his right hand. It signifies a prudent wife and illustrious person.
7. Arises a beautiful woman standing naked. It denotes a man of proud mind.
8. Ascends a sorrowful woman sitting upon a footstool. It signifies a man of low humble dejected spirit.
9. Ariseth a man holding a whip in his hand feeding sheep and goats in a field. The man then born will be neat-herd or shepherd.
10. Ascends two men standing, with a dog playing between them. It signifies an idle person, much addicted to venerous acts.

32. Second Decan of Taurus

Constellation: Perseus

Planet:: (Chaldean) Mercury

Element: Earth

Read comments in 1st decan above concerning Earthy people. Here we can add it is a mercurial earth, which by refining has become a quiksilver liquid metal. A mercurial person has obscure hidden depth beneath an ordinary exterior.

Tarot 6 pentacles

"A person in the guise of a merchant weighs money in a pair of scales and distributes it to the needy and distressed. It is a testimony to his own success in life, as well as to his goodness of heart.

Divinatory Meanings: Presents, gifts, gratification another account says attention, vigilance now is the accepted time, present prosperity, etc. Reversed: Desire, cupidity, envy, jealousy, illusion."

(AO)
"The second face of Taurus is of the moon and it is a face of power, nobility, dignity and necessity over people. The second face of Taurus a tall man girt with a girdle, holding a key in his right hand"

(YJ)
"The second Decan in Taurus is a red-faced woman whose arms and lower lip are also red. She is pre-eminent as she stands on one foot holding a jar. She is always intent on eating and drinking, and delights in gard woods."

THE GOETIA:

(Day) Marbas, Great lion,

(Night) Focalor Man with gryphons wings

TESTAMENT OF SOLOMON

"I am called Sphendonaêl. I cause tumours of the parotid gland, and inflammations of the tonsils, and tetanic recurvation. If I hear, 'Sabrael, imprison Sphendonaêl,' at once I retreat.'"

DAY BY DAY (AO)

11. Arises a crow, standing on the ground. It demonstrates a covetous person
12. Arise two women standing hand in hand. It imports a benevolent well minded man
13. Ascends two women with staves, smiting and striking one another. It denotes a troublesome, contentious wrangling person.
14. Arises a man holding a staff in his hand: hereby is signified an appeaser of quarrels, or one restraining and bridling the contentious.
15. Ascends 7 fowls, flying in the air. It signifies an unstable, wavering minded man
16. Ascends a man riding on an ass. It denotes a sluggard, a man slow and tedious in all his actions
17. Ariseth a bull bound by the middle of a tree. It signifies a man much over-laden with daily labour.
18. Ascends two bulls fighting one against the other. It denotes a raging, furious man.
19. Ascends a woman pouring water out of one pot into another. It signifies a smooth tongued person.
20. Ascends two dogs, fighting. It demonstrates an envious person.

33. Third Decan of Taurus

Constellation: Orion

Planet: (Chaldean) Saturn or Uranus

Element:: Earth

Saturnine earth, so the heaviest, darkest kind of earth. Very solid, the earthiest part of earth, perhaps salt of the earth, as in the one who wields the scythe of saturn to reap the harvest.

Tarot: 7 Pentacles

"A young man, leaning on his staff, looks intently at seven pentacles attached to a clump of greenery on his right; one would say that these were his treasures and that his heart was there.

Divinatory Meanings: These are exceedingly contradictory; in the main, it is a card of money, business, barter; but one reading gives altercation, quarrels--and another innocence, ingenuity, purgation. Reversed: Cause for anxiety regarding money which it may be proposed to lend."

(ao)

"The third face is of Saturn, and it is a face of misery, slavery. Madness, necessity and baseness. In the third a decrepit old man leaning on a crutch, hangin down one arm, and having a wooden leg."

(yj)

"The last Decan in Taurus is a woman ... with a tender body. She has a bull's hump, and wears a garland bright with campaka-flowers. Her eyebrows are fair, and her girdle hangs to the end of her buttocks."

Goetia:

(Day) Valefor Lion with ass's head bellowing.

(Night) Vepar, a mermaid.

Testament of Solomon::

"I am called Sphandôr, and I weaken the strength of the shoulders, and cause them to tremble; and I paralyze the nerves of the hands, and I break and bruise the bones of the neck. And I suck out the marrow. But if I hear the words, 'Araêl, imprison Sphandôr,' I at once retreat."

day by day (ao)

21. There arises a Bear looking backwards. It signifies a wicked, malicious and wrathful person.

22. Ascend three men holding one another by the hands: the person signified hereby, ill be a love of peace and friendship.

23. Ascends a man falling backwards to the earth. It signifies a man unfortunate in all things.

24. Ascends a crooked man holding himself up upon his staff, It denotes a person weak and feeble in his actions.

25. A man standing upright, and holding a staff in his hand. It signifies a valiant man, strong and powerful in his deeds.

26. A man standing showing his hand. A peaceful person, or a peace maker is hereby signified.

27. There arises the similitude of a field of wheat or corn standing uncut. This ascension denotes a gatherer together, and heaper up of riches.

28. A woman leading a horse by the bridle. It denotes a person desirous to rule over others.

29. There ascendeth a woman leading an Asse with a bridle, or otherwise a woman leading a he-goat by the horns. Hereby signifies a woman that rules over her husband.

30. There ascends a fair beautiful building. Hereby is signified a person delighting to do pleasant and delectable deeds.

34. First Decan of Gemini

Constellation: Eridanus / The River

Planet: (Chaldean) Jupiter or Neptune

Element: Air

"Again they are much as their name implies, Air is the medium in which living things breathe, it is the medium for the carrying of sound: n speech could happen without it; it connects all things; it blows to and fro.

Hence those in whose charts one or more of these are prominent tend to stress communication in some way. They are inclined to reasoning, intelligent pursuits, working in the realm of ideas. They like to bring into connection thoughts, people or places. They tend to be unimpressed by extreme prudence or sensitivity to others. "air does not wish to be confined in underground caverns, nor to have its light freedom saturated by "water". It enjoys the leaping response of "fire". Their faults can be a lack of deep emotion and a tendency to occupy themselves too much with schemes and theories, Certain expressions are indicative - "ideas all in the air", "much hot air, "too air-fairy", "Blowing in and out".

Tarot: 8 Swords

"A woman, bound and hoodwinked, with the swords of the card about her. Yet it is rather a card of temporary durance than of irretrievable bondage.

Divinatory Meanings: Bad news, violent chagrin, crisis, censure, power in trammels, conflict, calumny; also sickness. Reversed: Disquiet, difficulty, opposition, accident, treachery; what is unforeseen; fatality."

(AO)

"The first face of gemini is of Jupiter and is a face of writing, of giving and receiving money, of petitions, and wisdom in unprofitable things. The first face ascends like a young man girt with a girdle"

(YJ)

"The first Decan in the third sign carries a bow, and his hand is bright with arrows. He is adorned with a garland of many colours, and his necklace is pendant. The instruments of his craft are prepared. He knows how to use swords and missiles, and he wears a diadem and armour."

GOETIA:

(Day) Amon, wolf with serpent's tail or man with dog's teeth and raven's head.
(Night) Sabnock, Soldier with lion's head riding a pale horse.

TESTAMENT OF SOLOMON:

And the Seventh said: "I am called Sphandôr, and I weaken the strength of the shoulders, and cause them to tremble; and I paralyze the nerves of the hands, and I break and bruise the bones of the neck. And I, I suck out the marrow. But if I hear the words, 'Araêl, imprison Sphandôr,' I at once retreat."

DAY BY DAY (AO)

1. Ascendeth two men sitting on the ground holding one another by the hands. It signifies a joyful merry man.

2. There ascends one man girt with a sword, leading two other naked men bound. The person hereby signified will be a tailor or Thief taker.

3. Ariseth a man singing and playing on a lute. It denotes a man, causing joy to others

4. Ascends a man leading his wife by the hand. It signifies, one keeping good hospitality and entertainment for others,

5. A man holding a crossbow in his left hand, and a girdle in his right. It signifies a man preparing for war.

6. A man holding a balance in his right hand. It signifies a merchant.

7. Two brides, hand in hand. It denotes a person employed in nuptial affairs.

8. Ascends a smit smithing on iron, and a woman standing by idle. It signifies a person shunning labour, and loving idleness.

9. Ascends a king sitting on a throne, having a globe in his right hand and a scepter in his left. Signifying a man shall have great power and authority, that is born under this degree.

10. A man ascends lifting up another man from the ground. It signifies a person composing differences, friendly, amongst others.

35. Second Decan of Gemini

Constellation: Auriga

Planet: (Chaldean) Mars, or Moon

ELEMENT: AIR

The comments of air given in the previous entry, refined with the idea of martian air. The planet mars has very little atmosphere. Martian air would be very hot and thin, perhaps a person or entity given to hyperventilation, which makes the head swim and a red mist appear before the eyes, beware.

TAROT: 9 SWORDS

"One seated on her couch in lamentation, with the swords over her. She is as one who knows no sorrow which is like unto hers. It is a card of utter desolation.

Divinatory Meanings: Death, failure, miscarriage, delay, deception, disappointment, despair. Reversed: Imprisonment, suspicion, doubt, reasonable fear, shame."

(AO)

"The second face is of mars and is a face of burden, pressure, labour, and getting goods by labour, and of dishonest actions. The second is like a man with an axe cutting wood"

(YJ)

"The second Decan in Gemini is a black woman whose girdle is beautiful and whose garments are brightly coloured. She delights in the arts, in singing, and in story-telling. Holding a lyre, she is pleased and delighted. Her brows are lovely, and she is graceful."

GOETIA:

(Day) Barbatos, duke accompanied by four noble kings and great troops.
(Night): Shax, Stock-dove with sore throat.

TESTAMENT OF SOLOMON:

And the eight said: "I am called Belbel. I distort the hearts and minds of men. If I hear the words, 'Araêl, imprison Belbel,' I at once retreat."

DAY BY DAY (AO)

11. An eagle fluttering with her wings over three of her young ones. The man will be a south sayer or conjurer that is signified thereby.
12. Arise two women standing weeping. It signifies a sorrowful person.
13. Three crowns standing together in the group. It denotes a covetous and envious person
14. Ascends two foxes devouring hens. The man born under this degree, will be a glutton and covetous.
15. Ascends a man having three heads. It signifies one of good understanding.
16. Ascends like a bridge beside the water. It signifies a man labouring without profit.
17. Ascends a man without hands and idle. It signifies an unprofitable person.
18. A fix running swiftly. It denotes a laborious person.
19. Ascends a poor man carrying a staff on his shoulder. It signifies a man will be a travailler, a foot-post.
20. Three snakes lying on the ground. The man born under this degree will be wise and of good standing

36. Third Decan of Gemini

Constellation: The Enemy or Serpent

Planet: (Chaldean) Sun, otherwise Mars

Element: Air

See above comments of Air, here the solar air, like the solar wind which is invisible until it comes into contact with the earth's atmosphere when it transforms into the fantastic northern lights. So a person or entity needful of special circumstances in order to shine, but when they do, the results can be spectacular.

Tarot: 10 Swords

A prostrate figure, pierced by all the swords belonging to the card.

Divinatory Meanings: Whatsoever is intimated by the design; also pain, affliction, tears, sadness, desolation. It is not especially a card of violent death. Reversed: Advantage, profit, success, favour, but none of these are permanent; also power and authority.

AO

"The third face is of the sun, and is a face of oblivion, disdain, of mirth and jollity, and of hearing unprofitable words. The third, a man with a Hawk in his right hand, and a pipe in his left."

YJ

"The third Decan in Gemini wears red clothes and a red, pendant necklace. He is pale with red limbs, violent and fierce. The tip of his staff is red (with blood). He is the chief of a multitude of men. He bears a sword and missiles."

Goetia

(Day) Paimon, Crowned king on a dromedary accompanied by many musicians.

(Night) Viné, Lion on black horse carrying a viper

Testament of Solomon:

And the ninth said: "I am called Kurtaêl. I send colics in the bowels. I induce pains. If I hear the words, 'Iaôth, imprison Kurtaêl,' I at once retreat."

Day by Day (AO)

21 ascends a man sitting on horseback. It signifies a client or one retaining to another to have his defence.

22. Ascends two birds chattering together. It signifies a fowler.

23. A decrepit old man leaning on a staff. It demonstrates a more miserable idle person.

24. Two women sitting at play together. It represents one given to mirth.

25. A man holding a book open in his hand. It denotes a studious person.

26. Ascends two dogs fighting. It represents a quarelson litigious person.

27. A woman's ascends standing idle and weeping. An idle vagabond is hereby signified.

28. Ascend two bulls one greater than the other. A laborious man is hereby represented.

29. Three dogs, two running one way together, the other in a contrary way. The man thereby signified will be a huntsman to some nobleman.

30. Ascend two men each of them leading a hound in a chain, It signifies a hunstmans of a prince.

1. First Decan of Cancer

Constellation Sirius

Planet: (Chaldean) Venus, otherwise Moon

Element: water

Can be negative, Emotional, Unstable, Sensitive.

"Water reflects, dissolves, washes away helps growth. The sea has plumbable depths and holds much within it. It can be a calm exterior which can be deceptive since sudden storms blow up, and hidden undercurrents can drag down.

Water has no shape of its own. It takes on the shape of its container, Once contained iit can be calm and useful, but often damping. As a rushing torrent, it can be overwhelming and destructive, It has great carrying power and force if properly contained or canalised. This is best exemplified by the fixed sign scorpio.

Those with one or other of these signs prominent in their charts have a certain distrust of self. They need someone to reflect. They are happier when their fluidity is given shape by someone else, they are naturally sensitive and are the carriers of intuition and inspiration which they can express in such ways as rhythms of art or poetry, music, dancing or in the exercise of the psychic faculties. They are deep, emotional, secretive, [protective.

They tend to dislike people who are boisterous or who have strong personalities, finding them turing. Water feels that fire will make it boil and air will make it evaporate, but earth will contain it.

Their faults can be that they are literally "unstable as water", too easily being a reflection of the last persona they were with, too inclined to emotional storms, too ready to be a drag on others by subversive actions, too sensitive to influence. Slang words are aptly descriptive of the water nature: "sloppy" "wet" a wet blanket" a drip, No one is all water and the less desirable tendencies may be balanced elsewhere."

Tarot: 2 cups

A youth and maiden are pledging one another, and above their cups rises the Caduceus of Hermes, between the great wings on which appears a lion's head. It is a variant of a sign which is found in a few old examples of this card. Some curious emblematical meanings are attached to it, but they do not concern us in this place. Divinatory Meanings: Love, passion, friendship, affinity, union, concord, sympathy, the interrelation of the sexes, and--as a suggestion apart from all offices of divination--that desire which is not in Nature, but by which Nature is sanctified.

(AO)

"The first face of cancer is of Venus and is a face of joy, subtlety, humanity, Courtesy and of such things as induce men to love. The first face appeareth like a beautiful woman holding a flower in her hand." (AO)

(YJ)

"The first Decan in the fourth sign is a woman whose words are beautiful and full of grace. Holding a lotus in her hand, she stands in the water. Pining with love, she is as pale and fair as a campaka-flower. She wears a single white garment."

Goetia

(Day) Buer, centaur or archer.
(Night) Bifrons, a monster

Testament of Solomon:

The tenth said: (Day) "I am called Metathiax. I cause the reins to ache. (Night) If I hear the words, 'Adônaêl, imprison Metathiax,' I at once retreat."

Day by Day (AO)

1. Ascendeth a man and a woman holding one another by the hands and rejoicing. It signifies an amiable person given to mirth.
2. Ascends two women standing idle like two turrets. The man signified hereby will be idle
3. Arise two women sitting and two men standing before them. It signifies a serving man, ne waiting up another's pleasure
4. A maid standing idle, expecting a man. It represents a libidinous person full of lustful thoughts.
5. A woman standing expecting a man, It denotes a luxurious person.
6. A man holding a goat in a brass pot. It denotes a fool.
7. A man leading a goat with a girdle about his horns. A hangman is hereby dignified.
8. Ascends a house and a woman standing as it were absconding herself behind it. Signifies a lazy, slow and lascivious person
9. A woman holding a distaff in her right hand. It imports a laborious person.
10. A man holding a chest in his right hand signifies also a laborious person.

2. Second Decan of Cancer

Constellation : Procyon or second dog

Planet: (Chaldean) Mercury , or Mars

Element: Water

The remarks on the water element given in the previous entry in addition to the idea of Water of Mercury. In alchemy, mercury is considered to be a union of water and air, the liquid aspect of mercury, which once revealed remains ever so and does not revert to its previous solid state ever, except in exceptional circumstances. The planet mercury is closest to the sun and any physical water there would boil away although even in this harsh environment, frozen water ice exists. So contradictions.

Tarot: 3 Cups

"Maidens in a garden-ground with cups uplifted, as if pledging one another. Divinatory Meanings: The conclusion of any matter in plenty, perfection and merriment; happy issue, victory, fulfilment, solace, healing, Reversed: Expedition, dispatch, achievement, end. It also signifies the side of excess in physical enjoyment, and the pleasures of the senses.

AO

"The second face of cancer is of mercury and is a face of jollity, mirth, of women, of riches and plenty. It is a man and a woman sitting at a table with great heaps of money before them."

YJ

"The second Decan in Cancer is a girl seated on a snake-throne, having a medium form (?) and beauty. Her nature abounds in politeness and affection. Her body, adorned with jewels, is beautiful, and her garments are of a pale hue."

Goetia:

(Day) Duke like xenophon.

(Night) Uvall, Camel.

Testament of Solomon: The eleventh said: "I am called Katanikotaêl. I create strife and wrongs in men's homes, and send on them hard temper. If any one would be at peace in his home, let him write on seven leaves of laurel the name of the angel that frustrates me, along with these names: Iae, Ieô, sons of Sabaôth, in the name of the great God let him shut up Katanikotaêl. Then let him wash the laurel-leaves in water, and sprinkle his house with the water, from within to the outside. And at once I retreat."

Day by Day (AO)

11. A ship standing in the water signifies a fisherman
12. A man carrying the skin of a beast on his shoulders. A cobbler or or currier or such handicraft is hereby signified.
13. A boy sitting holding a book open with a pen in his hand. A studious person.
14. A lambe ascends having a crown of gold on his head. A gold smith
15. Ascends a house and a mouse lying on her nest under the roof there signifies a man desirous to keep his home.
16. A bird holding a serpent under her feet, It imports a man accounting himself noble.
17. A woman standing diel ascends. It signifies a sluggish person
18. Ascends a woman sitting at play at tables, A joyful. Merry person is represented.
19. A man having a spear in his right hand and a pipe in his left. A stage player is hereby signified,
20. A dog sitting in a chariot, signifies a slothful person.

3. Third Decan of Cancer

Constellation: Ursa Minor

Planet: (Chaldean) Moon otherwise Jupiter

Element: water

See previous comments on water. Here in lunar form, cool water is the medium by which the spirits of the otherworld travel through the biosphere, returning from the moon to the earth via the rain. A person or entity may have deep connections with those who came before and other realms.

Tarot 4 cups

A young man is seated under a tree and contemplates three cups set on the grass before him; an arm issuing from a cloud offers him another cup. His expression notwithstanding is one of discontent with his environment.

Divinatory Meanings: Weariness, disgust, aversion, imaginary vexations, as if the wine of this world had caused satiety only; another wine, as if a fairy gift, is now offered the wastrel, but he sees no consolation therein. This is also a card of blended pleasure. Reversed: Novelty, presage, new instruction, new relations.

AO

"The third face of cancer is of the moon, and is a face of hunting, pursuing fugitives, of getting goods of war, quarrels and contention amongst men. A hunter blowing a horn with a dog by his side and a spear on his shoulder."

YJ

"The third Decan in the fourth sign is set down as a woman who is the colour of a dark blue lotus and is pleasing to the eyes. Her upper-garment is of silk and (adorned with) bright jewellery. She is barren, but puffed up with pride in her beauty."

Goetia:

(Day) Sitri: Prince with leopard's head and gryphon's wings.
(Night) Haagenti, Bull with gryphon's wings

Testament of Solomon

The twelfth said: "I am called Saphathoraél, and I inspire partisanship in men, and delight in causing them to stumble. If any one will write on paper these names of angels, Iacô, Iealô, Iôelet, Sabaôth, Ithoth, Bae, and having folded it up, wear it round his neck or against his ear, I at once retreat and dissipate the drunken fit."

Day by Day (AO)

21. A chariot standing empty denotes a person devoted to vanity
22. Ascends a man standing idle, sinfies a slothful person.
23. Ascends running water, an unstable, unconstant person is signified.
24. Horses, one leaping on the other's back. It represents a man aspiring
25. A horse running in a field signifies an unstable person
26. A water springing out of mountains signifies a moveable unstable man.
27. A horse bridled signifies a man in bondage and servitude.
28. Ascends two men sitting under a tree and see a hawk in the tree. It denotes an idle person.
29. A man hanging on a gallows, signifies a thief.
30. A ship sailing in the water signifies a sailor or marriner.

4. First Decan of Leo

Constellation: Ursa major

Planet : (Chaldean) Saturn, or Sun

Element: fire
So elements of fire again but coming with subtle differences. Positive Ardent and Keen

In this traditional method of ascribing meaning to each of the three decans of the month, much use is made of the planetary influences. So the first decan of Aries will be of fire but of a martial quality. So heat of aggression and swift violence, The second decan of aries would be solar fire, which can also be relently if unrelieved by shade, And finally Jupitarian fire which is the warmth in the earth that causes things to grow and prosper.

"All three have something in common. All three have something of the nature of fire which actively burns, crackles, consumes, warms, delights or annoys according to whether it is suitably placed or not. It is delightful in the hearth, obnoxious of causing damage where it should not be burning.

Hence all people with one or more of these signs strong in their charts are active, ardent, enthusiastic, aspiring, emotionally able to burn with excitement or feeling of any kind, to become noisy actually or metaphorically, to have strong appetites for life, to be overpowering in consuming their less forceful companions, to be inflamed with the warmth which they bring to any interest, to delight when not in congenial company, They tend to be impatient of more sensitive or gentler people , thinking them slow or damping. "fire" feels that "water will extinguish it, and "earth" will smother it, but that "air" will fan its flames.

They are cheerful, gay, fond of sport and the joy of easer pulsating life. Their possible faults are those of being too lively , often rushing rashly into over-excitable, over-vividm unthoughtful, hence harmful or destructive ways. But no one is all Fire, and such tendencies may be balanced elsewhere in a chart.

Tarot: 5 wands

A posse of youths, who are brandishing staves, as if in sport or strife. It is mimic warfare, and hereto correspond the

Divinatory Meanings: Imitation, as, for example, sham fight, but also the strenuous competition and struggle of the search after riches and fortune. In this sense it connects with the battle of life. Hence some attributions say that it is a card of gold, gain, opulence. Reversed: Litigation, disputes, trickery, contradiction.

AO

"The first face of Leo is of Saturn and is a face of cruelty and violence and of sustaining great labours , boldness and lust. 1. It ascends like a man riding a lion. With a feather in his hat."

YJ

"The first Decan in Leo has a belly and a body like a lion's. He is fierce, armed with a sword, and arrogant with his mighty strength. His deeds are terrible and cruel, and he desires spicy foods. His fingers are many."

Goetia:

(Day) Beleth, King riding on a pale horse, with many musicians. Flaming and poisonous breath. (Night) Crocell, Angel

Testament of Solomon:

The thirteenth said: "I am called Bobêl (sic), and I cause nervous illness by my assaults. If I hear the name of the great 'Adonaêl, imprison Bothothêl,' I at once retreat."

day by day (AO)

1. A man holding a lion's head in his hand signifies a valiant man.
2. A ship. One side thereof inclining towards the waters signifies man unfortunate in the water.
3. A man ascends sitting mourning upon a foot-stool signifies a sorrowful person.
4. A fish swimming in the water, a prudent and a crafty person is her signified, affected by great men.
5. A serpent wreathed on the ground, signifies an envious person
6. A man holding a sword drawn in his right hand. A litigious person desirous to resist others is signified by this degree.
7. Ariseth a man riding upon a lion., a valiant man, strong and wise is denoted.
8. A fire flaming, it imports a labourer with fire.
9. A well clothed and adorned manit signifies a proud man,
10. Death, standing with a scythe in his hands. It signifies a murderer.

5. Second Decan of Leo

Constellation: Argo "The Ship"

Planet: (Chaldean) Jupiter

Element: Fire, as with previous comments, expansive fire with a tendency to get a little bit out of control. But also benign, as in the white heat of technology.

Tarot: 6 Wands

A laurelled horseman bears one staff adorned with a laurel crown; footmen with staves are at his side. Divinatory Meanings: The card has been so designed that it can cover several significations; on the surface, it is a victor triumphing, but it is also great news, such as might be carried in state by the King's courier; it is expectation crowned with its own desire, the crown of hope, and so forth. Reversed: Apprehension, fear, as of a victorious enemy at the gate; treachery, disloyalty, as of gates being opened to the enemy; also indefinite delay.

AO

"The second face is of Jupiter and is a face of wrangling, quarellings, ignorance, necessity of victory over the miserable and vile, through their ignorance and occasion of drawing swords and wars. The second is a man holding a sword drawn over his head in one hand, and a buckler in the other."

YJ

"The second Decan in Leo is bold and has loosened hair. She is on a mountain peak, proud of taking away the wealth of others. Terrible she causes . . . ; her actions are like those of a monkey."

Goetia

(Day) Leraje, an archer in green.

(Night) Furcas, Knight, cruel and ancient with long white hair and beard, rides a pale horse with sharp weapons.

Testament of Solomon

The fourteenth said: "I am called Kumeatêl, and I inflict shivering fits and torpor. If only I hear the words: 'Zôrôêl, imprison Kumentaêl,' I at once retreat."

Day by Day (AO)

11. A woman standing and showing her naked belly. It demonstrates an impudent immodest person
12. A beautiful woman ascends well adorned. It signifies a chast modest person
13. A bull feeding in pasture, it signifies a man constant and stable in his deeds.
14. A man standing idle ariseth, it signifies a loiterer.
15. A dog, or lion lying couched in the grass. A valiant man is hereby represented.
16. A bridled ass, an illiterate dull person is signified
17. Ascends a camel standing the person hereby signified will be valiant and full of spirit.
18. A key of a chamber, a man of power it imports
19. A man leading a horse by the bridle, it signifies a client or one pertaining to a nobleman,
20. A man holding a roll of paper in his hand. A messenger or carrier it signifies.

6. Third Decan of Leo

Constellation: Hydra

Planet: (Chaldean) Mars

Element: Martian Fire, can be the fire of war or maybe the heat of sexuality. So ardent and hot blooded.

Tarot 7 Wands

"A young man on a craggy eminence brandishing a staff; six other staves are raised towards him from below. Divinatory Meanings: It is a card of valour, for, on the surface, six are attacking one, who has, however, the vantage position. On the intellectual plane, it signifies discussion, wordy strife; in business--negotiations, war of trade, barter, competition. It is further a card of success, for the combatant is on the top and his enemies may be unable to reach him. Reversed: Perplexity, embarrassments, anxiety. It is also a caution against indecision.

AO

"The third face is of mars and is a face of love, society not parting from, not losing of one's own, for avoiding quarrels. The third is a young man with a hawk on his fist."

YJ

"The third Decan in Leo is a woman whose actions are marvellous and who is cunning in respect to machines and to undertakings involving the arts, business, or jewels. Seated on an ivory throne, she considers (?) the murder of her enemies."

Goetia:

(Day) Eligos, A night with a lance and banner, with a serpent.

(Night) Balaam, King with three heads: bull-man-ram, snakes' tail, flaming eyes riding a bear, carrying a goshawk.

Testament of Solomon

The fifteenth said: "I am called Roêlêd. I cause cold and frost and pain in the stomach. Let me only hear the words: 'Iax, bide not, be not warmed, for Solomon is fairer than eleven fathers,' I at [once] retreat."

DAY BY DAY

21. A man carrying a key in his hand. It signifies a keeper of good hospitality
22. A man lying as if he were dead. It signifies a weak, feeble person.
23. Ascends a man having two heads. It signifies a man of several minds.
24. A man holding a lock in his right hand. It signifies a man meditating wisdom
25. A man swimming in the water. It denotes a fisherman
26. A man working a dungfork. A labourer
27. A man holding a sickle in his right hand. A laborious person
28. Three men sporting together. It represents an idle fellow.
29. A man and a woman holding one another by the hands. An amiable person is signified
30. A servant riding a horse, The man signified will be a servant unto others

7. First Decan of Virgo

Constellation: Crater : The cup

Planet: (Chaldean) Sun

Element: Earth
Practical, Cautious

Again they are as the traditional name implies. From this comes the phrase "he is of the earth" The phrase "down to earth" is explanatory also "down to bedrock.

Earth is solid, dependable for support, motionless, dry, in modern idiom "functional" and rather uninteresting. No one is all "earth", but those in whose charts one or more of these signs are prominent have these traits of solid dependable, practicality. They are capable and hard working in sensible was, either in actual building or the building of careers and organisations.

They are careful and trustworthy with possessions or finance and will look after the small matters which make the complete whole. They tend to be suspicious or dubious about more lively agile-minded people, thinking them disturbing and trivial.

Earth feels "air" will dry it, "fire will parch it but that water will refresh it.

Their faults are liable to be that in their customary applications to material ends, they lack knowledge of the more abstract and inspirational things of life and may be thought dull by livelier people. Their faults can be narrowness of outlook, and too close addictions to order and to routine. Certain expressions are indicative - "He's rather a clod." No one is all Earth and such tendencies may be balanced elsewhere in the chart.

Tarot: 8 disks

An artist in stone at his work, which he exhibits in the form of trophies.

Divinatory Meanings: Work, employment, commission, craftsmanship, skill in craft and business, perhaps in the preparatory stage. Reversed: Voided ambition, vanity, cupidity, exaction, usury. It may also signify the possession of skill, in the sense of the ingenious mind turned to cunning and intrigue.

(AO)

"The first face of Virgo is of the sun and is a face of sowing, plowing, of planting herbs, gathering together riches and food. In the first face ascends a man laying money into a chest."

(YJ)

"The first portion of Virgo is a black man who possesses a subtle knowledge of crafts and who knows the rules of calculating, cleverness, and storytelling. He is attached to beauty and skill, and is determined in his purpose."

Goetia:

(Day) Zepar, soldier in red apparel and armour.
(Night) Alloces, Soldier with red leonine face and flaming eyes, rides a great horse,

Testament of Solomon:

The sixteenth said: "I am called Atrax. I inflict upon men fevers, irremediable and harmful. If you would imprison me, chop up coriander1 and smear it on the lips, reciting the following charm: 'The fever which is from dirt. I exorcise thee by the throne of the most high God, retreat from dirt and retreat from the creature fashioned by God.' And at once I retreat."

DAY BY DAY (AO)

1. Ascends a woman adorned expecting the sight of a man. It signifies a lover, either man or woman
2. Two women standing idle signifies a vagabond and idle person
3. A man holding a book of accounts in his hand signifies a merchant
4. A man at plow with oxen, a labourer in a field, signifies.
5. An eagle resting. A merchant but one living without labour is here signified.
6. A woman well clothed standing idle, signifies a idle person
7. A simple woman standing idle it signifies a sluggish person
8. A man sitting under a tree denotes a shepherd.
9. Ascends a woman well clothed with a red face standing idle. The man signified will be angry and luxurious
10. A man clothed standing idle holding an apple in his hand. It intimates a vagabond or wanderer about

8. Second Decan of Virgo

Constellation: Corvus "The Crow"

Planet: (Chaldean) Venus or Saturn

Element: Earth
As commented above, this is venusian earth, which is the warm fecund power within the earth, without which nothing can grow.

Tarot: 9 disks
A woman, with a bird upon her wrist, stands amidst a great abundance of grapevines in the garden of a manorial house. It is a wide domain, suggesting plenty in all things. Possibly it is her own possession and testifies to material well-being. Divinatory Meanings: Prudence, safety, success, accomplishment, certitude, discernment. Reversed: Roguery, deception, voided project, bad faith.

(AO)
"The second face is of venus and is a face of gain, of getting, substance, covetously raking together, of being covetous and arising with the strength of men. In the second two men, one having a purse in his hand."

(YJ)
"The second Decan in the sixth sign is a beautiful woman whose limbs are polluted by her menstruation. She loves a man in secret for the sake of a child. She is learned; striving on behalf of the people, she journeys to a foreign country."

Goetia:
(Day) Botis, Viper or human with teeth and to horns and with a sword (Night) Camio, A thrush or a man with a sharp sword seems to answer in burning ashes or coals of fire.

Testament of Solomon

The seventeenth said: "I am called Ieropaêl. On the stomach of men I sit, and cause convulsions in the bath and in the road; and wherever I be found, or find a man, I throw him down. But if any one will say to the afflicted into their ear these names, three times over, into the right ear: 'Iudarizê, Sabunê, Denôê,' I at once retreat."

Day by Day (AO)

11. A white horse bridled running. The man hereby signified will be swift of foot.
12. A man in red clothes with a black face represents a wicked person
13. Two woman gathering roses a merry jocund man denotes
14. An ox standing in a pasture. The man born under this degree will be laborious.
15. Two merry women standing together signifies a merry person.
16. Ascends two dogs running together the man having this degree will be a huntsman.
17. A fair castle compassed about with a hedge signifies a man living in safety.
18. Ariseth a tree full of leaves standing in grass. Signifies a man laboured with his words.
19. A man sitting as a servant upon a horse. Will be a retainer to another.
20. Ariseth a bird following a mole or a mouse signifies a man contrary to others.

9. Third Decan of Virgo

Constellation: Coma

Planet:: Mercury

ELEMENT: EARTH
As commented above but now the mercurial earth, meaning the metallic ore that when processed yields its secret from.

TAROT: 10 DISKS
A man and woman beneath an archway which gives entrance to a house and domain. They are accompanied by a child, who looks curiously at two dogs accosting an ancient personage seated in the foreground. The child's hand is on one of them.

Divinatory Meanings: Gain, riches; family matters, archives, extraction, the abode of a family. Reversed: Chance, fatality, loss, robbery, games of hazard; sometimes gift, dowry, pension.

(AO)
"In the third face of Virgo is of mercury and is a face of old age, of debility, slothfulness and of loss of the members through infirmities, of pulling up trees, and depopulation of places peopled, In the third a decrepit old man leaning on a staff."

(YJ)
"The third Decan in Virgo is a woman who is naturally coquettish and graceful. Her face is smiling, her countenance moon-like. Her one braid of hair is adorned with adoka-flowers, and her steps seem to stumble with intoxication. "

Goetia

(Day) Bathin, a strong man with a serpent's tail, on a pale horse.

(Night) Murmur, warrior with ducal crown rides gryphon accompanied by trumpeters.

Testament of Solomon:.

The eighteenth said: "I am called Buldumêch. I separate wife from husband and bring about a grudge between them. If any one write down the names of thy sires, Solomon, on paper and place it in the ante-chamber of his house, I retreat thence. And the legend written shall be as follows: 'The God of Abram, and the God of Isaac, and the God of Jacob commands thee -- retire from this house in peace.' And I at once retire."

day by day (AO)

21. A man ariseth standing and holding gold in his right hand and silver in his left signifies a rich man
22. A named woman carrying a goat and a lamb on her shoulders, an impudent immodest person it denotes.
23. A man ascends rowing a boat in the water with an oar signifies a mariner.
24. A bird bound by the neck to a post signing a man who will be restrained and held to labour.
25. A man casting a stone into a ditch signifies a litigious person.
26. Two men discoursing together signifies the man will be well educated.
27. Two women standing idle denotes an idle person.
28. Ascends some on the ground, some flying in the air signifies a man shall have much rent.
29. Ascends dew or rain falling on the ground, a person will be religious.
30. Ascends a dumb man standing still signifies a fool.

10. First Decan of Libra

Constellation : Centaur

Planet: (Chaldean) Moon or Venus

Element: Air
Keywords: Positive Intellectual, Communicative

"Again they are much as their name implies, Air is the medium in which living things breathe, it is the medium for the carrying of sound: n speech could happen without it; it connects all things; it blows to and fro.

Hence those in whose charts one of more of these are prominent tend to stress communication in some way. They are inclined to reasoning, intelligent pursuits, working in the realm of ideas. They like to bring into connection thoughts, people or places. They tend to be unimpressed by extreme prudence or sensitivity to others. "air does not wish to be confined in underground caverns, nor to have its light freedom saturated by "water". It enjoys the leaping response of "fire". Their faults can be a lack of deep emotion and a tendency to occupy themselves too much with schemes and theories. Certain expressions are indicative – "ideas all in the air", "much hot air, "too air-fairy", "Blowing in and out".

Tarot 2 swords
A hoodwinked female figure balances two swords upon her shoulders.

Divinatory Meanings: Conformity and the equipoise which it suggests, courage, friendship, concord in a state of arms; another reading gives tenderness, affection, intimacy. The suggestion of harmony and other favourable readings must be considered in a qualified manner, as Swords generally are not symbolical of beneficent forces in human affairs. Reversed: Imposture, falsehood, duplicity, disloyalty.

(AO)

"The first face of Libra is of the moon and is a face of justice, right and truth, of succouring the weak against the strong and the wicked and of helping the poor and miserable. A student having a book open before him." .

(YJ)

"The first Decan in Libra is a man in the market place with the implements of his trade prepared. His limbs are covered with silk and bright ornaments; his body is black and his eyes beautiful. His places are where there is gold, merchandise, mines, and treasure."

GOETIA

(Day) Salos, soldier with ducal crown riding a crocodile.
(Night) Orobas, Horse

TESTAMENT OF SOLOMON

The nineteenth said: "I am called Naôth, and I take my seat on the knees of men. If any one write on paper: 'Phnunoboêol, depart Nathath, and touch thou not the neck,' I at once retreat."

DAY BY DAY (AO)

1. ascendeth a man holding in each hand a spear, signifies a warrior
2. A clergyman with a pot of incense signifies a religious person
3. A decrepit man crooked in his hands and feet signifies a miserable laborious person
4. A man at play with horses, signifies a labourer in the fields
5. A black bird with a red bill and feet denotes a fat gross person
6. A man drawing a plow himself signifies a man taking a great deal of pains without sense or reason
7. A man holding a gold ring in his right hand signifies a lover

8. a woman weeping over one that is sick dignifies a sorrowful man
9. A man holding a sword over his head in his right hand signifies a litigious person
10. A black bird holding his beak to the ground signifies to be altogether a slover.

11. Second Decan of Libra

Constellation: Bootes

Planet: (Chaldean) Saturn or Uranus

Element: Air

As with above comments on the element, but this is Saturnine air, so a certain restriction of air, or shortness of breath.

Tarot: 3 swords

Three swords piercing a heart; cloud and rain behind.

Divinatory Meanings: Removal, absence, delay, division, rupture, dispersion, and all that the design signifies naturally, being too simple and obvious to call for specific enumeration. Reversed: Mental alienation, error, loss, distraction, disorder, confusion.

(AO)

"The second is of Saturn and is a face of quietness, plenty, and a good life, quiet and secure. An old man in a gown sitting in a chair."

(YJ)

"The second Decan in Libra is a fair-waisted woman who has learned a little of the crafts. She wears bright garments and a bright, pendant necklace. She is clever in the office of an intermediary (between lovers) for the sake of the bridegroom. Her actions are like those of rogues and cheats."

Goetia

(Day) Purson, Lion faced man riding a bear, carrying a viper, trumpeter with him.

(Night) Gremory, Beautiful woman, with duchess crown tied to her waist, riding a great camel.

Testament of Solomon

The twentieth said: "I am called Marderô. I send on men incurable fever. If any one write on the leaf of a book: 'Sphênêr, Rafael, retire, drag me not about, flay me not,' and tie it round his neck, I at once retreat."

Day by Day (AO)

11. A man with black hands and face but white feet denotes an idle, dull but unstable person
12. A woman standing looking about her. The man having this ascendant will be a vagabond and idle
13. A man and a woman going two several ways denotes a contentious man who lives divided from others
14. A great looking glass, fixed upon a wall denotes a proud person.
15. Two hearts hanging together signifies a worldling.
16. A camel running signifies the will will be swift and valiant.
17. A bird sweetly singing signifies a person full of mirth.
18. Ascends the similitude of a village neatly build signifies a man having domination in the country
19. A fair castle on a mountain denotes a noble man.
20. A fair altar beautifully adorned signifies a religious man.

12. Third Decan of Libra

Constellation : The Cross

Planet: (Chaldean) Jupiter or Mercury

Element: Air

See previous comments, but Jupitarian air wants to expand and fill the space, so the very opposite of shortness of breath, the lungs are filled to capacity giving great strength and capacity to the body.

Tarot 4 swordsThe effigy of a knight in the attitude of prayer, at full length upon his tomb. Divinatory Meanings: Vigilance, retreat, solitude, hermit's repose, exile, tomb and coffin. It is these last that have suggested the design. Reversed: Wise administration, circumspection, economy, avarice, precaution, testament.

(AO)

"The third face of of Jupiter and is a face of gluttony, of sodomy, of singing and mirth and folllwing evil pleasures. It's face is a young man with a cup in his hand."

(YJ)

"The third Decan in Libra is a man about to attack. The tops of his teeth are far apart, and the hair on his body is long. . . . He carries a bow and wears armour and a turban. He engages in the tricks of rogues."

Goetia

(Day) Marax, Human faced bull.
(Night) Osé, Leopard.

TESTAMENT OF SOLOMON

The twenty-first said: "I am called Alath, and I cause coughing and hard-breathing in children. If any one write on paper: 'Rorêx, do thou pursue Alath,' and fasten it round his neck, I at once retire..."

DAY BY DAY (AO)

21. A man riding on an ass or horse will be a horseman or a groom or servant.
22. A horse saddled. A man coveting much and enjoying little
23. A physician viewing am urinal through a glass, The man will be a physician
24. Ascends a man in the upper part and a horse in the lower parts, beating a dragon with a staff signifies a strong man.
25. Peacock standing in the grass signifies a proud person
26. A man beating a lion with a staff signifies he will be a conqueror in war
27. A shady tree standing in a garden signifies a man to be a gardiner.
28. A man labouring with a spade, pretends to be a laborious person.
29. A woman standing idle signifies an idle person
30. A hare running out of a wood signifies someone inconstant and unstable.

13. First Decan of Scorpio

Constellation: Animal held by centaur

Planet:: Mars

Element: Water

Negative, Keywords Emotional, Unstable, Sensitive

"Water reflects, dissolves, washes away helps growth. The sea has plumbable depths and holds much within it. It can be a calm exterior which can be deceptive since sudden storms blow up, and hidden undercurrents can drag down.

Water has no shape of its own. It takes on the shape of its container, Once contained iit can be calm and useful, but often damping. As a rushing torrent, it can be overwhelming and destructive, It has great carrying power and force if properly contained or canalised. This is best exemplified by the fixed sign scorpio.

Those with one or other of these signs prominent in their charts have a certain distrust of self. They need someone to reflect. They are happier when their fluidity is given shape by someone else, they are naturally sensitive and are the carriers of intuition and inspiration which they can express in such ways as rhythms of art or poetry, music, dancing or in the exercise of the psychic faculties. They are deep, emotional, secretive, [protective.

They tend to dislike people who are boisterous or who have strong personalities, finding them turing. Water feels that fire will make it boil and air will make it evaporate, but earth will contain it.

Their faults can be that they are literally "unstable as water", too easily being a reflection of the last persona they were with, too inclined to emotional storms, too ready to be a drag on other by subversive actions, too sensitive to influence. Slang words are aptly descriptive of the water nature: "sloppy" "wet" a wet blanket" a drip, No one is all water and the less desirable tendencies may be balanced elsewhere."

Tarot 5 Cups

A dark, cloaked figure, looking sideways at three prone cups, two others stand upright behind him; a bridge is in the background, leading to a small keep or holding.

Divinatory Meanings: It is a card of loss, but something remains over; three have been taken, but two are left; it is a card of inheritance, patrimony, transmission, but not corresponding to expectations; with some interpreters it is a card of marriage, but not without bitterness or frustration. Reversed: News, alliances, affinity, consanguinity, ancestry, return, false projects.

(AO)

"The first face of scorpio is of mars and is a face of strife, sadness, deceit, detraction, perdition and treachery In the first face appears two men fighting and tearing one another by the hair."

(YJ)

"The first Decan in the eighth sign is a blazing man whose staff is fierce to his enemies. His sword is drawn, his armour is of gold; his flames are fanned by anger. He sports with serpents whose poison is sharp."

Goetia

(Day) Ipos, angel with lion's head, goose's feet, hare's tail.
(Night) Amy, Flaming fire

TESTAMENT OF SOLOMON

Rhyx Audameoth who inflicts heart pain for the 22nd

DAY BY DAY (AO)

1. A man holding a spear in his hand signifies a thief and a wicked fellow
2. A man riding an elephant denotes a valiant and stable person.
3. A man standing idle declares a person to be wicked and idle.
4. A man playing a harp denotes a joconde merry man.
5. A man ascends wanting the lower part of his body will be imperfect in his deeds.
6. An ass or horse led and saddled signifies a man producing few things to good effect.
7. A man sitting and having a purse of his money in his right hand and in his let a golden cup denotes a rich merchant
8. A great cock standing, the man will be a scribe.
9. A man sitting in a tub denotes one of little wit.
10. A head with a face much wrinkled signifies a man of strange opinions

14. Second Decan of Scorpio

Constellation: Northern crown

Planet (Chaldean) Jupiter or Neptune

Element: water

so see comments on water above with added refinement of expansive, Jupitarian water. Water cannot be compressed, it can only expand, so irrepressible.

Tarot: 6 cups

Children in an old garden, their cups filled with flowers.

Divinatory Meanings: A card of the past and of memories, looking back, as--for example--on childhood; happiness, enjoyment, but coming rather from the past; things that have vanished. Another reading reverses this, giving new relations, new knowledge, new environment, and then the children are disporting in an unfamiliar precinct. Reversed: The future, renewal, that which will come to pass presently.

(AO)
"The second face is of the sun and is a face of affronts, detections, stirring up mschiefs and quarrels between men and continuing that strife which it stirreth up. The second a man sitting on a stool, and two dogs fighting by him."

(YJ)
"The second Decan in Scorpio is a woman with loose hair who is bound with snakes. She is robbed by thieves in the forest. With black body and completely naked she runs swiftly from a bandit, calling out terribly and shrilly."

Goetia

(Day) Aim, Man with three heads, a serpent;s, a man (having two stars on his brow, and a calves. Rides a viper and bears a firebrand.

(Night) Oriax, Lion on horse, with serpent's tail, carries in right hand two hissing serpents.

Testament of Solomon

The twenty-third said: "I am called Nefthada. I cause the reins to ache, and I bring about dysury. If any one writes on a plate of tin the words: 'Iathôth, Uruêl, Nephthada,' and fasten it round the loins, I at once retreat."

Day by Day (AO)

11. A man holding scorpion by the neck signifies an envious person
12. A great serpent with three flies biting her. A wise but wicked man
13. A fair and strong tower, the man will be a strong labourer.
14. A well without water signifies a man with unstable wit.
15. A fair woman standing idle, denotes an idle person
16. A woman giving alms to a poor man signifies a merciful man.
17. A wolf running in a field denotes a robber.
18. A house and a woman hiding herself behind the door signifies a sluggish idle person
19. A dog with great mouth and ears represents a noble person
20. A man sitting on a camel signifies a noble person

15. Third Decan of Scorpio

Constellation The serpent held by Ophiuchus

Planet: (Chaldean) Venus or Moon

ELEMENT: WATER
Water of Venus, which would be very hot, almost boiling.

TAROT: 7 CUPS
Strange chalices of vision, but the images are more especially those of the fantastic spirit. Divinatory Meanings: Fairy favours, images of reflection, sentiment, imagination, things seen in the glass of contemplation; some attainment in these degrees, but nothing permanent or substantial is suggested. Reversed: Desire, will, determination, project.

(AO)
"The last Decan in the eighth sign is a cruel man wearing a golden suit of armour. Standing in a hole, he is clever (in obtaining) treasure and what he desires (?). He wishes to follow a vow that is broken. He knows how to use weapons, but is tormented, having been robbed by his companions."

(YJ)
"The third face is of Venus and is a face of war, drunkenness and violence, fornication, wrath and pride. In the third, two women pulling one another by the hair of the head, one having a staff in her right, striking the other on the head."

GOETIA
(Day) Naberius, A black crane with a sore throat, fluttering.
(Night) Vapula, Lion with gryphon's wings

TESTAMENT OF SOLOMON

The twenty-fourth said: "I am called Akton. I cause ribs and lumbic muscles to ache. If one engraves on copper material, taken from a ship which has missed its anchorage, this: 'Marmaraôth, Sabaôth, pursue Akton,' and fasten it round the loin, I at once retreat."

DAY BY DAY (AO)

21. A horse standing freely in a field signifies a man shall not be subject to the yoke of others.
22. A great flood of water denotes an unstable person
23. Man rivers flowing out of a fountain signifies an unstable, unconstant person
24. A woman holding a distaff (of wool) in her right hand signifies a laborious man.
25. A wolf carrying a foul in his mouth signifies a thief and a robber
26. A man carrying garments spoiled on his shoulder signifies as destroyer
27. Two men standing speaking together signifies a jocund sociable person
28. A house or great church signifies a man much given to praying
29. A master sitting with a book open signifies a studious mn
30. A serpent with a great head is a prudent person.

16. First Decan of Sagittarius

Constellation : Ophiuchus

Planet Chaldeanmercury alt Jupiter

Element: Fire

Positive Keywords Ardent, Keen

In this traditional method of ascribing meaning to each of the three decans of the month, much use is made of the planetary influences. So the first decan of Aries will be of fire but of a martial quality. So heat of aggression and swift violence, The second decan of aries would be solar fire, which can also be relently if unrelieved by shade, And finally Jupitarian fire which is the warmth in the earth that causes things to grow and prosper.

"All three have something in common. All three have something of the nature of fire which actively burns, crackles, consumes, warms, delights or annoys according to whether it is suitable or not. It is delightful in the hearth, obnoxious of causing damage where it should not be burning.

Hence all people with one or more of these signs strong in their charts are active, ardent, enthusiastic, aspiring, emotionally able to burn with excitement or feeling of any kind, to become noisy actually or metaphorically, to have strong appetites for life, to be overpowering in consuming their less forceful companions, to be inflamed with the warmth which they bring to any interest, to delight when not in congenial company, They tend to be impatient of more sensitive or gentler people , thinking them slow or damping. "fire" feels that "water will extinguish it, and "earth" will smother it, but that "air" will fan its flames.

They are cheerful, gay, fond of sport and the joy of easer pulsating life. Their possible faults are those of being too lively , often rushing rashly into over-excitable, over-vividm unthoughtful, hence harmful or destructive ways. But no one is all Fire, and such tendencies may be balanced elsewhere in a chart.

Tarot: 8 wands

The card represents motion through the immovable-a flight of wands through an open country; but they draw to the term of their course. That which they signify is at hand; it may be even on the threshold.

Divinatory Meanings: Activity in undertakings, the path of such activity, swiftness, as that of an express messenger; great haste, great hope, speed towards an end which promises assured felicity; generally, that which is on the move; also the arrows of love. Reversed: Arrows of jealousy, internal dispute, stingings of conscience, quarrels; and domestic disputes for persons who are married.

(ao)

"The first face is of mercury and is a face of boldness, freedom and warfare. Ascendeth a man armed with a polax."

(yj)

"The first Decan in Sagittarius is a man whose bow is drawn and whose speed is as violent as a horse's. He has knowledge of chariots and weapons, and bears the instruments for the sacrifice. His body is protected by gold, and his earrings flash with gold."

Goetia

(Day) Glasya-Labolas A dog with a gryphon's wings.
(Night) Zagan, Bull with gryphon's wings

TESTAMENT OF SOLOMON

The twenty-fifth said: "I am called Anatreth, and I rend burnings and fevers into the entrails. But if I hear: 'Arara, Charara,' instantly do I retreat."

DAY BY DAY (AO)

1. Three men standing without heads signifies a man will be religious and just.
2. A man shooting an arrow out of a crossbow signifies a person always litigious.
3. 1 man sitting on a ram clothes with flame signifies a litigious troublesome person
4. A man carrying a spear on his shoulder, signifies a destroyer
5. A woman carrying s cradle on her shoulder denotes a laborious person
6. An ox with three horns signifies a man of good understanding
7. A woman standing idle. The man signified hereby will be an idle person
8. Two men playing at dice upon a table signifies a player
9. A great fire of wood burning denotes a man will be a labourer with fire.
10. A portion of gold and silver in the earth signifies a rich man

17. Second Decan of Sagittarius

Constellation: Hercules

Planet: (Chaldean) Moon or Mars

ELEMENT: FIRE

As above but now lunar fire, which must be a very cool, healing kind of fire, like burning camphor

TAROT: 9 WANDS

The figure leans upon his staff and has an expectant look, as if awaiting an enemy. Behind are eight other staves--erect, in orderly disposition, like a palisade.

Divinatory Meanings: The card signifies strength in opposition. If attacked, the person will meet an onslaught boldly; and his build shews, that he may prove a formidable antagonist. With this main significance there are all its possible adjuncts--delay, suspension, adjournment. Reversed: Obstacles, adversity, calamity.

(AO)

"The second face is of the moon and is a face of fear or lamentation, grieff and of a fearful spirit over his own body"

(YJ)

"The second Decan in Sagittarius is a woman who is charming, graceful, and beautiful. She is seated on an auspicious throne, and is pale with a golden-hued body. Opening a golden casket in a heap of jewels, she takes pleasure in distributing (its contents)."

Goetia

(Day) Bune, Dragon with three heads, a dog's, a man's and gryphon's.
(Night) Volac. Child with angel's wings rides a two-headed dragon

Testament of Solomon

The twenty-sixth said: "I am called Enenuth. I steal away men's minds, and change their hearts, and make a man toothless (?). If one writes: 'Allazoôl, pursue Enenuth,' and tie the paper round him, I at once retreat."

Day by Day (AO)

11. An ape sitting upon a wolf signifies a ruler over another man,
12. A man riding upon a goat signifies a contrarier of others.
13. A man having his hands bound behind him signifies a conquered vanguised man
14. A master holding a book open, the man signified will be learned..
15. A man walking by a horse saddle signifies a fearful coward.
16. Chariot wheels without the body signifies a man void of reason
17. A decrepit person leaning on a staff signifies a man much given to prayer
18. A man holding a bird by the tail and on the other hand a burning torch signifies a man will be a fowler.
19. A house comassed about with burning faggots. The man thereby signified will be laborious and compassed about with fear.
20. Three men walking leaning one another by the arms signifies one merry and sociable.

18. Third Decan of Sagittarius

Constellation: The Eagle

Planet: (Chaldean) Saturn or Sun

ELEMENT: FIRE
Slow burning, with a tendency to go out.

TAROT 10 WANDS
A man oppressed by the weight of the ten staves which he is carrying.

Divinatory Meanings: A card of many significances, and some of the readings cannot be harmonized. I set aside that which connects it with honour and good faith. The chief meaning is oppression simply, but it is also fortune, gain, any kind of success, and then it is the oppression of these things. It is also a card of false-seeming, disguise, perfidy. The place which the figure is approaching may suffer from the rods that he carries. Success is stultified if the Nine of Swords follows, and if it is a question of a lawsuit, there will be certain loss. Reversed: Contrarieties, difficulties, intrigues, and their analogies.

(AO)
"The third face of Saturn is a face of willfulness and not being persuaded from it, of contraying, yielding, agility in evil, strife and horrible things. In the third is a man with a feather in his hat, holding a staff on top of his finger."

(YJ)
"The third Decan in Sagittarius is a bearded man with a black body. Clothed in silk and pining with love, he is graceful. On his breast hangs a string of pearls, and a bracelet is on his upper arm. He desires music and perfume."

GOETIA

(Day) Ronove, A monster, possibly a makara.

(Night) Andras, Angel with raven's head. Rides black wolf, carries sharp sword.

TESTAMENT OF SOLOMON:

The twenty-seventh said: "I am called Phêth. I make men consumptive and cause hemorrhagia. If one exorcise me in wine, sweet-smelling and unmixed by the eleventh aeon1, and say: 'I exorcise thee by the eleventh aeon to stop, I demand, Phêth (Axiôphêth),' then give it to the patient to drink, and I at once retreat."

DAY BY DAY (AO)

21. A man standing in the habit of a doctor denotes a wise man
22. Two men piercing one another with their swords signifies a thief and manslayer
23. A woman cutting another in the breast with a knife signifies a manslayer
24. A man running himself through with a sword signihes a man that will be his own enemy
25. A man vomiting upon the ground signifies a drunkard yet a laborious man
26. A man playing with a little staff will be a stage player, a merry person.
27. A man hanging with his hands on a beam denotes a merry fellow
28. A man riding on a camel signifies a valiant man
29. A man tumbling himself out of one bed and into another signifies a childish man,
30. A man holding a horse hoof in his hand signifies a black smith

19. First Decan of Capricorn

Constellation: Ara, the altar

Planet: Saturn

Element: Earth
keywords practical, Cautious

Again they are as the traditional name implies. From this comes the phrase "he is of the earth" The phrase "down to earth" is explanatory also "down to bedrock.

Earth is solid, dependable for support, motionless, dry, in modern idiom "functional" and rather uninteresting. No one is all "earth", but those in whose charts one or more of these signs are prominent have these traits of solid dependable, practicality. They are capable and hard working in sensible ways, either in actual building or the building of careers and organisations.

They are careful and trustworthy with possessions or finance and will look after the small matters which make the complete whole. They tend to be suspicious or dubious about more lively agile-minded people, thinking them disturbing and trivial.

Earth feels "air" will dry it, "fire will parch it but that water will refresh it.

Their faults are liable to be that in their customary applications to material ends, they lack knowledge of the more abstract and inspirational things of life and may be thought dull by livelier people. Their faults can be narrowness of outlook, and too close addictions to order and to routine. Certain expressions are indicative - "He's rather a clod." No one is all Earth and such tendencies may be balanced elsewhere in the chart.

Tarot: 2 Disks

A young man, in the act of dancing, has a pentacle in either hand, and they are joined by that endless cord which is like the number 8 reversed.

Divinatory Meanings: On the one hand it is represented as a card of gaiety, recreation and its connexions, which is the subject of the design; but it is read also as news and messages in writing, as obstacles, agitation, trouble, embroilment. Reversed: Enforced gaiety, simulated enjoyment, literal sense, handwriting, composition, letters of exchange.

(AO)

"The first face is of Jupiter and is a face of wandering, of travaile, of joy, of gain and loss, with weakness and vileness. In the first face ascends a man travailing on foot."

(YJ)

"The first Decan in Capricorn is the colour of collyrium. His teeth are as terrible as a crocodile's. He is armed with a staff, and his actions are like those of Time and Death. He stands in the middle of a cemetery with an armour of heavy hair and a strong body."

Goetia

(Day) Berith, gold crowned soldier in red on a red horse, bad breath.
(Night) Haures, Leopard

Testament of Solomon

The twenty-eighth said: "I am called Harpax, and I send sleeplessness on men. If one write 'Kokphnêdismos,' and bind it round the temples, I at once retire."

Day by Day (AO)

1. Two men in like form signifies a joconde amiable person

2. A man carrying a redd on his shoulder ... a man without power
3. A great serpent ascends her by signifying a wise man.
4. two rakes in a field signifies a clown
5. Two gates open signifies a man given to hospitality
6. A man carrying two dogs on his shoulder signifies a litigious person
7. A man standing between two woman denotes a merry person
8. A hand holding a bird a fowler represents
9. A man falling on the ground denotes a feeble person
10. A man with a lapwing in each hand s fowler or hunter signifies.

20. Second Decan of Capricorn

Constellation: Draco, the serpent

Planet: (Chaldean) Venus

Element: Earth
As above but also Venusian earth, as in warm and fructifying.

Tarot 3 Pentacles
A sculptor at his work in a monastery. Compare the design which illustrates the Eight of Pentacles. The apprentice or amateur therein has received his reward and is now at work in earnest.

Divinatory Meanings: Métier, trade, skilled labour; usually, however, regarded as a card of nobility, aristocracy, renown, glory. Reversed: Mediocrity, in work and otherwise, puerility, pettiness, weakness.

(AO)
"The second face is of mars and is a face of seeking such things as cannot be known; and seeking after such things as cannot be attained to. In the second a man reaching at a bird in the air."

(YJ)
"The second Decan in Capricorn is a man of blazing splendour whose teeth are dark blue and like a Pisaca's [a type of demon]. He is handsome, having bound on his armour, sword, and turban (sirastrina). He wanders about constructing river-embankments, tanks, and aqueducts."

Goetia
(Day) Astaroth, Hurtful angel on an infernal dragon with a viper, bad breath.
(Night) Andrealphus, Noisy peacock

Testament of Solomon

The twenty-ninth said: "I am called Anostêr. I engender uterine mania and pains in the bladder. If one powder into pure oil three seeds of laurel and smear it on, saying: 'I exorcise thee, Anostêr. Stop by Marmaraô,' at once I retreat."

Day by Day (AO)

11. A king crowned receiving letters from a messenger, is signified will be an ambassador to a prince
12. A man running swiftly denotes a swift person
13. A man carrying a goates skin on his shoulders, a hangman represents
14. A hand holding a spear imports a litigious troublesome person
15. A man bending his knees denotes a noble person
16. A man riding an unbridled horse signifies a man without power
17. A man with a dog's head signifies a man full of strife.
18. A man divided in one half denotes a pusillanimous childish person
19. A man having four legs standing idle signifies a man playing or resting when he should be at work
20. an ape looking at himself in a glass denotes a proud man.

21. Third Decan of Capricorn

Constellation: Sagitta "The Arrow"

Planet: (Chaldean) Mercury

Element: Earth

Again as other comments on Mercurial earth, the rich elemental ore from which when refined gives rise to a mysterious healing substance.

Tarot: 4 disks

A crowned figure, having a pentacle over his crown, clasps another with hands and arms; two pentacles are under his feet. He holds to that which he has.

Divinatory Meanings: The surety of possessions, cleaving to that which one has, gift, legacy, inheritance. Reversed: Suspense, delay, opposition.

(AO)

"The third face is of the sun, and is a face of covetousness, of governing one substance, of not sufficing himself and of suspecting. In the third a man is sitting at a table telling of money."

(YJ)

"The third Decan in Capricorn is a woman with loose hair, a gaping mouth, and a hanging belly. Her red body is tall and thin. She holds a noose in her hand, and wears a winding-sheet. She delights in injury."

Goetia

(Day) Forneus, Sea Monster.
(Night) Cimejes, warrior on black horse.

TESTAMENT OF SOLOMON

The thirtieth said: "I am called Alleborith. If in eating fish one has swallowed a bone, then he must take a bone from the fish and cough, and at once I retreat."

DAY BY DAY (AO)

21. A master holding a book open signifies a learned man,
22. A man digging the ground with a spade a labourer represents
23. A man leading a woman by the hand a lover denotes
24. A cooper working on a cask signifies am artificer
25. A man with a hawk on his hand signifies a noble man
26. A fair grove of trees the man signified will be a labourer inwoods
27. A man lying on the grass a weak feeble person signifies
28 A man carrying earth on his head denotes a rich man
29. A fair woman sitting on a stool signifies a man full of mirth
30. The tail of a fish signifies a man imperfect in his deeds

22. First Decan of Aquarius

Constellation: Aquila "The Falling Eagle"

Planet: (Chaldean) Saturn or Uranus

Element: Air
Positive

Again there are much as their name implies, Air is the medium in which living things breathe, it is the medium for the carrying of sound: speech could happen without it; it connects all things; it blows to and fro."

Hence those in whose charts one of more of these are prominent tend to stress communication in some way. They are inclined to reasoning, intelligent pursuits, working in the realm of ideas. They like to bring into connection thoughts, people or places. They tend to be unimpressed by extreme prudence or sensitivity to others. "air does not wish to be confined in underground caverns, nor to have its light freedom saturated by "water". It enjoys the leaping response of "fire". Their faults can be a lack of deep emotion and a tendency to occupy themselves too much with schemes and theories, Certain expressions are indicative - "ideas all in the air", "much hot air, "too air-fairy", "Blowing in and out".

Tarot: 5 swords
A disdainful man looks after two retreating and dejected figures. Their swords lie upon the ground. He carries two others on his left shoulder, and a third sword is in his right hand, point to earth. He is the master in possession of the field.

Divinatory Meanings: Degradation, destruction, revocation, infamy, dishonour, loss, with the variants and analogues of these. Reversed: The same; burial and obsequies.

(AO)

"The first face is of venus and is a face of an anxious spirit grieving after gain, and never resting, of labour, loose, poverty and vileness. The first face is a woman sitting on a rock."

(YJ)

"The first Decan in Aquarius is a man who has dreadful teeth. He knows how to practise magic. His is the colour of a dark cloud, and half of his hair is filthy. His actions are pitiless. Garbed in an antelope-skin, he has the nature of one who is not insignificant."

Goetia

(Day) Foras, a strong man in human shape.
(Night) Amdusias, Unicorn or dilatory band master.

TESTAMENT OF SOLOMON

The thirty-first said: "I am called Hephesimireth, and cause lingering disease. If you throw salt, rubbed in the hand, into oil and smear it on the patient, saying: 'Seraphim, Cherubim, help me!' I will retire at once."

DAY BY DAY (AO)

1. A man holding in each hand a bird signifies a fowler
2. A man holding both his hands on his head signifies a sorrowful person
3. A man holding one hand upon his head signifies a man full of grief
4. A man riding on his treasure a merchant denotes
5. A women going before and a man following her denotes a solicitous person
6. A man playing with a staff signifies a merry person
7. A sword drawn lying on the ground a soldier or warlike person it represents

8. A man holding a chain in his hand signifies a man not enjoying himself

9. One man lifting up another from the ground denotes an idle person

10. A man standing with a head denotes a man without power

23. Second Decan of Aquarius

Constellation: Delphinus The Dolphin (Egypt: a water vessel)

Planet: (Chaldean) Mercury

Element: Air

All the things said earlier are elements of Air but also a mercurian quality, when the cinnabar ore is heated the mercury escapes as a gas which when cooled become the liquid mercury we know. So mercurial vapour would be a very toxic kind of air.

Tarot: 6 swords

A ferryman carrying passengers in his punt to the further shore. The course is smooth, and seeing that the freight is light, it may be noted that the work is not beyond his strength. Divinatory Meanings: journey by water, route, way, envoy, commissionary, expedient. Reversed: Declaration, confession, publicity; one account says that it is a proposal of love.

(AO)

"The second face is of mercury And is a face of beauty, understanding, humanity, modesty, good manners, compliments and freedom. The second a comely person well clothed sitting on a stool."

(YJ)

"The second Decan in Aquarius is a man with a shining sword. Half of his hair is tawny. Covered with garlands of skulls, he wears armour. His is the colour of sunset-clouds, and his protruding teeth are fierce. He is covered with the strings of nooses and so forth."

Goetia

(Day) Asmoday, King with three heads, (bull, man, ram) snakes tail, goose's feet, rides with lance and banner on a dragon.

(Night) Belial, Two beautiful angels sitting in a chariot of fire.

Testament of Solomon

The thirty-second said: "I am called Ichthion. I paralyze muscles and contuse them. If I hear 'Adonaêth, help!' I will retire at once."

day by day (ao)

11. An armed man without a head signifies a noble man without power
12. An armed man smiting down a king signifies someone who will be ruler over a king {rhis serves a comment in italic)
13. A troop of horsemen armed denotes a litigious person and a robber
14. A man holding a boot in his hand represents a sorrowful person
15. Two men riding on a unicorn denotes a litigious person
16. A man holding fire in his hand denotes a labourer with fire
17. A woman lying sick a bed an infirm and idle person is represented,
18. A great owl standing still denotes an envious man
19. A man holding another's head in his hand denotes a man having power and authority
20. A decrepit woman leaning on a staff a weak feeble person signifies

24. Third Decan of Aquarius

Constellation: Southern Fish

Planet: Venus

Element: Air.
As with he entry for first decan of Aquarius with added refinement of Venusian air, which might be the potentially romantic words, which are things carried by the air, carrying a romantic quality, but still a little technical.

(ao)
"The third face is of the moon and is a face of direction and affronts. The third man having an envious look with his hands on his sides.

(yj)
"The third Decan in Aquarius is a man with various weapons wearing a garland of golden Moons. His shape is boar-like, his form frightful. Producing red (sandalwood?) in his garden (or Mount Malaya), he is an ascetic whose hair is reddish-brown like a monkey's."

Tarot: 7 swords
A man in the act of carrying away five swords rapidly; the two others of the card remain stuck in the ground. A camp is close at hand. Divinatory Meanings: Design, attempt, wish, hope, confidence; also quarrelling, a plan that may fail, annoyance. The design is uncertain in its import, because the significations are widely at variance with each other. Reversed: Good advice, counsel, instruction, slander, babbling.

Goetia
(Day) Gaap, Prelate guide to four kings.
(Night) Decarabia, A star in a pentacle

Testament of Solomon

The thirty-third said: "I am called Agchoniôn. I lie among swaddling-clothes and in the precipice. And if any one write on fig-leaves 'Lycurgos,' taking away one letter at a time, and write it, reversing the letters, I retire at once. 'Lycurgos, ycurgos, kurgos, yrgos, gos, os.' "

Lycurgos means "wolf's work". Name taken by Spartan lawmaker, perhaps at behest of oracle of Apollo at Delphi? An epithet of Apollo, "The Wolf God" . This method of constructing a spell from a word, reducing it letter by letter, has been in use a very long time.

day by day (AO)

21. A man clothed lying on his back on the ground an infirm man denotes
22. A man cutting off anothers hands and feet with a hatchet denoted a wicked doer,
23. Two dogs running together signifies a man given to sport
24. A man weeping holding his hand to his head signifies a man always sorrowful
25. One carrying a great spear a thief and wicked person signifies
26. Water flowing out of a great mountain sn undtablr unsettled man it represent
27. A house compassed about with a hedge signifies a man safe in his deeds.
28. A man drinking out of a vessel declared a joyful man
29. A man sitting on a horse back holding a sword drawn in his hand signifies a warrior
30. A king crowned sitting signifies a man living at peace.

25. First Decan of Pisces

Constellation: Pegasus

Planet: (Chaldean) Jupiter or Neptune

ELEMENT: WATER
Negative, Emotional, Unstable, Sensitive

"Water reflects, dissolves, washes away helps growth. The sea has plumbable depths and holds much within it. It can be a calm exterior which can be deceptive since sudden storms blow up, and hidden undercurrents can drag down.

Water has no shape of its own. It takes on the shape of its container, Once contained iit can be calm and useful, but often damping. As a rushing torrent, it can be overwhelming and destructive, It has great carrying power and force if properly contained or canalised. This is best exemplified by the fixed sign scorpio.

Those with one or other of these signs prominent in their charts have a certain distrust of self. They need someone to reflect. They are happier when their fluidity is given shape by someone else, they are naturally sensitive and are the carriers of intuition and inspiration which they can express in such ways as rhythms of art or poetry, music, dancing or in the exercise of the psychic faculties. They are deep, emotional, secretive, protective.

They tend to dislike people who are boisterous or who have strong personalities, finding them turing. Water feels that fire will make it boil and air will make it evaporate, but earth will contain it.

Their faults can be that they are literally "unstable as water", too easily being a reflection of the last persona they were with, too inclined to emotional storms, too ready to be a drag on others by subversive actions, too sensitive to influence. Slang words are aptly descriptive of the water nature: "sloppy" "wet" a wet blanket" a drip, No one is all water and the less desirable tendencies may be balanced elsewhere."

(AO)

"The first face of pisces is of and is a face of anxiety, of many thoughts, of journeys and removing from place to place, of seeking after substance and food. In the first ascends a man travailing, carrying a burden on his back."

(YJ)

"The first Decan in Pisces is a woman with a beautiful body whose eyes are expansive and long. Her body is adorned with silk and gold. She stands by the Great Sea, which she has crossed in a boat for the sake of a heap of jewels."

TAROT: 8 CUPS

A man of dejected aspect is deserting the cups of his felicity, enterprise, undertaking or previous concern.

Divinatory Meanings: The card speaks for itself on the surface, but other readings are entirely antithetical--giving joy, mildness, timidity, honour, modesty. In practice, it is usually found that the card shows the decline of a matter, or that a matter which has been thought to be important is really of slight consequence--either for good or evil. Reversed: Great joy, happiness, feasting.

Goetia

(Day) Furfur, Hart with a fiery tail, or an angel.

(Night) Seere, A beautiful man on a winged horse

TESTAMENT OF SOLOMON

The thirty-fourth said: "I am called Autothith. I cause grudges and fighting. Therefore I am frustrated by Alpha and Omega, if written down."

DAY BY DAY (AO)

1. Two men with one head joyed together dignified a troublesome and inconstant person.
2. A man sitting on the earth denotes a clown
3. A man eating a roll of bread will be a baker
4. A unicorn lying on his back denotes a man without power
5. Two maids standing together a merry person signifies
6. A great bird feeding on the ground a covetous miser represents
7. A man holding a bell in each hand denotes a sexton or keeper of a church
8. A man sitting in a tub with a brush in his hand signifies a maker of bathes
9. A pilgrim walking denotes a religious man
10. A man beating in a mortar signifies a laborious man.

26. Second Decan of Pisces

Constellation: Cygnus

Planet: Moon

Element: water
Lunar water, the moon said to control the tides, both on the earth and in a metaphysical sense. Water is the medium by which so-called dead souls re-enter the biosphere, ready for reincarnation. Intoxicating stuff.

Tarot: 9 cups
A goodly personage has feasted to his heart's content, and abundant refreshment of wine is on the arched counter behind him, seeming to indicate that the future is also assured. The picture offers the material side only, but there are other aspects.

Divinatory Meanings: Concord, contentment, physical bien-être; also victory, success, advantage; satisfaction for the Querent or person for whom the consultation is made. Reversed: Truth, loyalty, liberty; but the readings vary and include mistakes, imperfections, etc.

(ao)
"The second face of pieces is of Jupiter and is a face of praising oneself, of a high mind, of seeking after and intermingling with great and high things. The second, an ancient man pointing with his hand to the sky. "

(yj)
"The second Decan in Pisces is a woman dreadful in strife, the foremost one. She is fierce, and has no clothes; her colour is white, red, and black. Her garments and ornaments are destroyed; desiring clothes, she shouts out."

Goetia

(Day) Marchosias, Wolf with gryphon's wings and ser[ent's tail, breathing flames.

(Night) Dantalion, Man with many countenances, all men;s and women;s, carries a book in his right hand.

Testament of Solomon

The thirty-fifth said: "I am called Phthenoth. I cast evil eye on every man. Therefore, the eye much-suffering, if it be drawn. frustrates me."

day by day (AO)

11. A man walking with a staff on his arm signifies a vagabond
12. A young man looking behind him signifies a timorous person
13. A man and a woman rising on horseback denotes an idle person
14. A man cutting wood in a wood denotes a labourer.
15. A man with a knife drawn denotes a man preparing for strife
16. A man holding a cock in his hand signifies a noble man
17. A man drowning himself in the water signifies a senseless person
18. Two horse men fighting signifies a troublesome litigious man.
19. A man piercing himself through with a sword signifies someone who will be cause of their own death
20. A moon shining in the night signifies an unstable unconstant person

27. Third Decan of Pisces

Constellation: The Band or Bridle

Planet : Mars

ELEMENT: WATER.
All of the above, "fire water" perhaps, so doubly intoxicating.

TAROT 10 CUPS
Appearance of Cups in a rainbow; it is contemplated in wonder and ecstasy by a man and woman below, evidently husband and wife. His right arm is about her; his left is raised upward; she raises her right arm. The two children dancing near them have not observed the prodigy but are happy after their own manner. There is a home-scene beyond.

Divinatory Meanings: Contentment, repose of the entire heart; the perfection of that state; also perfection of human love and friendship; if with several picture-cards, a person who is taking charge of the Querent's interests; also the town, village or country inhabited by the Querent. Reversed: Repose of the false heart, indignation, violence.

(AO)
"The third face is of mars and is a face of fornication and embraces of great delight with women and loving peace and quietness. The third is a young man embracing a beautiful woman."

(YJ)
"The third Decan in Pisces is a woman whose hair has been loosened and who wears ornaments bearing the emblem of (the tribe of) abhiiras (cow?).* Ahirs or Yudav tribe of nomadic herdsmen, same lineage as Krishna) She shrieks, as she is frightened. She stands in the water adorned by troops of spirits having the shapes of jackals, cats, and boars."

Goetia

(Day) Stolas, A raven. Andromalius, Man holding great serpent

(Night) Andromalius, A man carrying a great serpent

Testament of Solomon:

The thirty-sixth said: "I am called Bianakith. I have a grudge against the body. I lay waste houses, I cause flesh to decay, and all else that is similar. If a man writes on the front-door of his house: 'Mêltô, Ardu, Anaath,' I flee from that place."

day by day (ao)

21. Two men stabbing one another signifies a man slayer
22. A woman having her garments rent denotes an immodest person
23. A soman swimming in a boat denotes an inconstant person
24. A man and a woman lying in a bed denotes a lascivious person
25. A man casting a stone into a ditch signifies a troublesome person
26. A woman cutting off a mans head with an axe as he lies asleep signifies a man slayer
27. A man standing naked pissing signifies an immodest person
28. A man walking by a horse holding in one hand a bird and in the other a serpent.
29. A great sidh out of the water signifies an unstable person.
30. A woman looking in a glass denotes a proud, unchaste person.

Decan	2020	2021	2022	2023	2024	2025
1	20-Jul	10-Jul	28-Jul	17-Jul	05-Jul	24-Jul
2						
3						
4	19-Aug	08-Aug	27-Aug	16-Aug	04-Aug	23-Aug
5						
6						
7	17-Sep	07-Sep	25-Sep	15-Sep	03-Sep	21-Sep
8						
9						
10	16-Oct	06-Oct	25-Oct	14-Oct	02-Oct	21-Oct
11						
12						
13	15-Nov	19-Nov	23-Nov	13-Nov	01-Nov	Nov-20
14						
15						
16	14-Dec	04-Dec	23-Dec	12-Dec	01-Dec	20-Dec
17						
18						
19		13-Jan	02-Jan	21-Jan	12-Jan	01-Jan
20						
21						
22		11-Feb	01-Feb	20-Feb	09-Feb	29-Jan
23						
24						
25		13-Mar	02-Mar	21-Mar	10-Mar	28-Feb
26						
27						
28		12-Apr	01-Apr	20-Apr	08-Apr	29-Mar
29						
30						
31		11-May	30-Apr	19-May	08-May	27-Apr
32						
33						
34		13-Jun	30-May	18-Jun	06-Jun	27-May
35						
36						
34			29-Jun			25-Jun
35						
36	Leap or Thoth month/decans when needed					

2026	2027	2028	2029	2030	Decan
14-Jul	04-Jul	22-Jul	11-Jul	30-Jul	1
					2
					3
12-Aug	02-Aug	20-Aug	10-Aug	29-Aug	4
					5
					6
11-Sep	31-Aug	18-Sep	08-Sep	27-Sep	7
					8
					9
10-Oct	30-Sep	18-Oct	Oct-07	26-Oct	10
					11
					12
09-Nov	29-Oct	16-Nov	Nov-06	25-Nov	13
					14
					15
09-Dec	28-Nov	16-Dec	Dec-05	24-Dec	16
					17
					18
18-Jan	7 Jan / 27 Dec		14-Jan	04-Jan	19
					20
					21
17-Feb	06-Feb	26-Jan	13-Feb	02-Feb	22
					23
					24
19-Mar	Mar-08	25-Feb	15-Mar	04-Mar	25
					26
					27
17-Apr	07-Apr	26-Mar	13-Apr	02-Apr	28
					29
					30
16-May	06-May	24-Apr	13-May	02-May	31
					32
					33
15-Jun	04-Jun	24-May	12-Jun	01-Jun	34
					35
					36
		22-Jun		30-Jun	34
					35
					36

Index

Symbols

12 days of Christmas 34

A

Aabt-offerings 84, 87, 122
Abramelin 55
Abydos 71, 76, 83, 102
Africa
  East 22
  Loango 22
  Massai 22
Age
  Neolithic 25
  Old 84, 108
  Primordial 74
Air 49
Akhw 9, 37, 74, 86, 87, 125, 134
Ambisexual 49
Amulets 130
Amun-Ra 49
Ancestor
  Father and mother 124
Andromalius 134
Andromeda 134
Anger 116
Ankh
  Ankhew 37
  Ankhew, Akhew & Neterew 37–38
Ankh-tawi 63
Anubis 62, 89, 98
  Feast of 126
Apophis 56, 75, 88, 96, 106, 120
  Archaic burial 66
Ashmunein 71, 85
Astrological Optics (book) 141
Astrology
  Modern Textbook of 139
Atum 87, 103

B

Baba/Babai 108
  Red eared Baboon 58
Babylon
  Lunar calendar 35
Bahr Yusuf 17
Banebdjedet 104
  The lusty bull 71
Bastet 39, 63, 71, 76, 80, 83, 84, 95
Bata
  Ears of 75
Beer 126
Benben 76
Betelgeuse 25
Birds 59, 112
Birth
  Conception 27
  Nine months 26
  Omen 106
Black 130
Blood 39
Blue lily 116
Boat 67
  Mandjet 60
  Mesektet 82, 124
  Neshmet 76
  Prow of 64
  Repulsion of the crew 123
Body
  Hand shaking 119
Book of Calamities 44
Book of Fate 44
Book of Nuit 47
Book of the Fundamentals of the
    Course of the Star 49
Borchardt, Ludwig 20
Bread 126
  And beer 65

Brugsch, Heinrich 20, 23
Bull
   Trampling of 56, 101, 119, 123
Bull of Ombos 16
Busiris 67, 97, 98

C

Cakes of light 38
Calendar
   Civil 16
   Gregorian 19
   Jewish 34
   Julian 32
   Lunar 16, 22, 24
      Southern 25
   Lunar double dates 18
   Lunar-Solar 25
   Lunar-Stella 20, 28
Cattle 90, 99
Cave 96
Chanting 82
Children
   Children of Bedesh (Apophis) 63, 66, 102, 120
   Children of Nut (epagomenal days) 114
   Of Geb and Nut 126
   Of the storm 71
Coffin 45
Constellations
   Cygnus 26
   Milky Way 27
   Orion 25, 57
Coptic 90
Crocodile 40, 56, 58, 66
Crowley, Aleister
   Gnostic Mass 5, 37
Culminating 41
Cygnus 28

D

Day
   Break 25
   Darkness 94
   Epagomenal 12, 130
Dead, the 94

Death
   In foreign lands 63
Decans 37, 40, 114, 235
   Ephemeris 50
   Orion 98
Decapitation 115
Deir el Bahri 25
Demon 39
   Hayety 39
   Shemay 39
Dendara 43, 45
Dep 68, 96, 110, 112
Depuydt, Leo 16
Disease & medicine 20, 83, 104
   Blindness 125
   Pestilence 71, 83
   Skin rash 62, 113
Dismemberment 70
Djed pillars 72, 87
Djesert 96
Dog 40, 82
Dolphin 79
Doomed Prince
   Tale of the 40
Drunkenness 63
   Feast of 35
Duat 27, 56, 57

E

Earth Mother 45
Ebers, George 20
El Lahun 17
Elephantine 31
Equinox
   Vernal 26
Executioners (flowercutters) 56, 88, 111
   Of Ra 84
   Seven 89
Eye
   Akhet 114, 117
   Fugitive 119
   Horus the Elder 99
   Of Horus 125
   Wedjat 62, 87, 99, 104, 112, 115, 125

F
Faiyum 17
Feasts/festivals
  Jubilation 62
  Of your god 125
Feeding
  The gods 121
Ferryman 70
Fire 49, 118
Fish 58, 59, 75, 79, 112
Flint 84
Flower
  Cutters 40

G
Geb 49, 98
Gemini 26
Ghosts 38
Glass 82
Goddess
  Four noble ladies 38
  Three noble ladies 73
Gods
  Fear of 39
  Flighting 115
  Local 9, 65, 86
  Minor 39
  Of the day 81
  Tying of the throats 115
Goetia 41, 134, 135, 141
Gold 78, 82
Green 130

H
Hapy 85
Harpoon 60
Hathor 39, 45, 56, 68, 76
  Counting by names 111
  Emissaries 40
  Great book of fate 39
  Seven 39, 40
  White one 105
Hatshepsut 25
Heart 38
Hedj-hotpe 76
Hefau 85

Heliopolis 25, 47, 63, 72, 87, 92, 93, 101, 103
Herbs 20
Honey 84
Horizon 25
  Doorways 73, 97
  Eastern 86
Horoscopes 44
Horus 11, 58, 60, 72, 89, 92, 105, 111, 129
  & Seth 58, 69, 73, 85
  Crown
    White 73
  Feast of 96, 104
  Fighting 13
  Hekenu 80
  The Elder 62, 98, 99, 118, 128
Horus & Seth 60
  Battlefield 85
  Fighting 92
House
  Foundation 67
  Holy 106, 127
  Of Ra 56, 104
House of Life *13*, 19
Houses 41
Hu/Hw 62, 81, 85, 128

I
Ibis 57, 71
Illahun 17, 19
Incense 85, 99, 111
Incubi 39
Ipet-hemet (Hippo) 116
Iron 72
Isis 11, 72, 89, 128, 129
Isis and Nephthys
  Lamentations 82

J
Judgement 93

K
Karnak 94
Khenti-irty 81, 88
Khepra 100

Khnum 93
Khonsu 39
King
  White crown 64

L

L. p. h. (life, prosperity and health 58, 99
Lesser Key of Solomon 135
Letopolis 11, 78, 89, 94, 107, 122, 123, 129
Lion 60, 66, 74, 78, 113, 114, 125
Lizards 65
Lyet 89

M

Maat 81, 87, 107, 119
  Navigation of 86
Magic
  Mistress of 11, 129
Mahes 80
Maner 123
Marduk 46
Masturbation 47
Medinat Habu 47
Megiddo 17
Menit 235
Mesektet 60, 72
Mesore 18
Midheaven 41
Milk 84
Milky Way 45
Min 90
  Feast 127
  Into the tent 99
Mithras 46
Mnevis 87
Month
  First day of 23
  Intercalary 34, 35, 51
  Lunar 22
  Synodic 23
Montu 63, 100
Moon
  Anomaly 24

Bio-dynamism 20
Conjunction 23
Dark or waning half 19
God 39
New 17, 23
  Determining 34
Old crescent 22
Musician
  Goddess 57
Mut
  In Shera 121
Myrrh 99

N

Nagada 25, 28, 32
Nefertem 80
Nehebkau 80
Neith 58, 62, 66, 76, 92, 114
  Letter writing 88
Nemty 70
Nephthys 12, *13*, 72, 128, 129
  Beautiful of face 129
Neterew 37
Nile 28
  First cataract 31
  High 55
Nuit 26, 27
  Milky Way 26
  Son of 100
  The Book of 49
  Who counts the days 95
Nun 65, 82, 85, 94
  His cavern 124

O

Oath 85
Observation 19
  Error 24
Omens
  In the sky 56
Onnophris 102, 103, 118
  In Sais 71
Osiris 16, 82, 87, 89, 110, 128
  Abydos 96
  Feast 65, 76
  Khenty 113

P

Papyrus Carlsberg 36
Papyrus Ebers 20, 21
Papyrus, Edwin Smith Surgical Papyrus 20
Papyrus Kahun 17
Parker, Richard 20, 24
Pawt-cake 81
Pesedjenet 17, 23
Portal 124
Priest 17
   Overseer of the hour 19
   Temple 39
Ptah 73, 80, 86, 127
Ptah-Sokar-Osiris 103

Q

Qadesh 17
Quartz 78

R

Ra
   Birth of 27
   Crew of 110
   Setting 102
   Sun god 26
Ra Horakhty 35, 55, 130
Ramesses II 35
Ramesses III 47
Rebellion 88, 94, 108, 112, 119
Red
   Goddess 99
Rennutet 72
Rostau 83, 123

S

Satet 31
Scepter
   Was 88
Seasons
   Peret 98
Sekhmet 60, 76, 81, 82, 85, 88, 102, 120
Serpent 72
Seth 11, *13*, 16, 60, 64, 65, 75, 86, 89, 124, 128, 129
   Confederates of 60, 86, 89, 100, 124
   Decapitation 64
   Desert land 73
   Name of 95, 102
   Red one 73
   Sw, Heracleopolitan nome 100
Sety I 41
Sex 39
   Homosexual 62
   Intercourse 63, 81
Shu 49, 72, 82, 114, 115
Sia 62, 81
Sky 45
   If you see anything 56, 60, 62, 67, 74, 75, 82, 84, 86, 87, 90, 92, 103, 114, 120
Smell 65, 99
Snake 5, 37, 40, 67, 125
   Fire spitting cobra 57
Sobek 58, 102, 106, 114
   Tongue of 66
Sokar 127
Solstice
   Summer orientation 25
   Winter 25, 26, 27
   Winter orientation 25
Son of Nwt 47
Songs 82
Sopdu (Sirius) 20, 25, 31, 32, 123, 164
   Heliacal Rising 25, 26, 28, 34, 51
Spirits (akhw) 65, 74, 79, 81, 87, 94, 102
   Holy Guardian Angel 37
Star
   70 days absence 31
   Apparent motion 24
   Goddess 44
   Going forth of 99
   Rigel 25
Stonehenge 24
Succubi 39
Sun

Midday 77, 127
Sw 100

T

Tanenet 73, 80
Tarot 140
Tefnut 49
Tekhen 35
Temhu 102
Temple
  Inaccessible 75
  Kri- shrines 114
  Ritual 94
Testament of Solomon 41, 141
Thoth 34, 35, 51, 62, 81, 85, 93, 107, 115
Tree 96
  Holy 63
Triplicities 50
Turqoise 70
Two Brothers
  Tale of 40

U

Underworld 41
Ursa Major *13*

V

Vampires 39
Violence 117
Voice
  Raising 91

W

Wabet 62, 65, 89
Weaving
  God 63
  Goddess 56, 76
Wind 40
Womb 45

Y

Yahweh 46
yavana jataka 141
Year
  365 day 31
  Eleven day interval 34, 51
  Leap 35
  Nineteen year cycle 35
  Opener of 32, 35
  Wandering 32

Z

Zodiac 2, 43

Decan image from Temple of Philae

Menit, which is a counterpoise for a heavy necklace associated with the goddess Hathor, here showing gods of the Decans in various registers. Staatliche Museum, Berlin.

www.ingramcontent.com/pod-product-compliance
Lightning Source LLC
Chambersburg PA
CBHW051122160426
43195CB00014B/2307